Exempt fr

MW01493647

Robert M. Collins

with Richard C. Doty and Timothy S. Cooper
as contributors and writers.

Peregrine Communications
865 Helke Road
Vandalia OH 45377

ISBN 0-9766426-3-8

© 2006 by Robert M. Collins
with Richard C. Doty and Timothy S. Cooper
as contributors and writers.

Second Edition

Revised 2008

Alien on cover is courtesy of Robert Dean

Table of Contents
Introduction

Section I: In The Beginning

Section II: Key Players

Section III: What Lies Beneath

Epilogue

INTRODUCTION

This book is not a history of UFOs nor does it make an attempt to be. A chronology is followed, but if the reader is looking for a comprehensive historical account there are a number of good books available. What we attempt to do in this book is to provide strong, supportive, and corroborating evidence in the form of photographs, drawings of facilities and "Eyes Only" sensitive documents to support the case for a UFO cover-up.

Two major elements seem to makeup the UFO mystery: The UFOs themselves and the intensive, concerted and single-focused efforts by the governments of the world to withhold information about them. Neither the nature nor the purpose of these governmental action's are clearly understood except perhaps for reasons of fear driven by politics and the general fear of the unknown. But this policy dates back to the latter part of World War II when UFO-like "foo-fighters" were being reported by combat pilots.

The trail for some started back in 1985, for others as far back as 1947, and for others even before. In 1985, Bill Moore (author of "Roswell" book), Jaime Shandera (Hollywood TV producer), Ernie Kellerstrass (retired Air Force Lt. Col. with an intelligence background), Rick Doty (USAF Counter-Intelligence), plus others and myself were brought together as a group attempting to uncover the truth. What is MJ-12 and who are some of these secret players like James Angleton, Allen Dulles, Richard Helms and Rick Doty not to mention those mysterious "Men-in-Black" who controlled so much of what we wanted to know, yet stood in contempt of the public's right to know? Did James Jesus Angleton or Allen Dulles have clues about who killed JFK? Were UFOs one of the prime reasons for the assassination in the first place? In Section 2, Chapters 1 and 2, we will attempt to answer those questions. Finally, where did the government hide many of these forbidden alien artifacts?

Was it at Wright-Patterson AFB, Los Alamos National Labs (LANL) or Area 51-S4 or all of the above? Then they proceeded to place those artifacts and the entire subject in "don't exist" categories. In Section 3 we will attempt to answer those questions.

Despite what many critics and debunkers say there is an enormous amount of circumstantial evidence that supports the reality of UFOs. Given the amount of circumstantial evidence it seems that fear is one of the primal driving forces behind much of the debunking and skepticism. What would happen if the public really knew we were faced with aliens claimed to be 20-25,000 years ahead of us? If they wanted to destroy us they would have already done so; if their motive is not to destroy us, then what? If all the source stories are true then we have large quantities of recovered alien technology hidden away waiting for the time for our technology to catch up to theirs. If true, then does the U.S. Government have some type of agreement that gives the alien visitors something for what we are supposedly receiving from them?

Our original goal was to never write any books, appear on any documentaries or TV shows or to become public figures in any way except for consulting work and running a Web site. We saw ourselves as a "behind the scenes" kind of people who would set up meetings between contacts, coordinate information and provide other support when needed. This book has the same title as the book Bill Moore and Jaime Shandera intended to publish, but for many reasons it never materialized. If it were not for the relentless persistent attitudes of many people, this book would have never come about, so our appreciation and thanks goes out to all of those unnamed people.

Trying to get information out of sources has turned into a real power struggle over the years since 1985. We would compare it to the turf battles that the 15 different intelligence agencies fight over with respect to their intelligence and intelligence gathering abilities according to the recently released 9/11 Commission Report at http://www.9-11commission.gov/. Sometimes there would be a flood of information, but at other times dead silence. Too often the information would be fed in bits and pieces then stopped. It was just enough to keep your interest, but not enough to do anything with. Even with sources there always seems to be a paranoid "fear factor" that controls every action combined with an attitude of "we have something that nobody else has." An interesting quote from *Cold Warrior* (a book on James Jesus Angleton) 1991 by Tom Mangold typifies just what UFO researchers are up against.

"Angleton learned on the job, quickly mastering the basic tools of counterintelligence, including the use of 'black' propaganda, and the vital ingredient known as 'playback'—understanding how effectively your own disinformation is actually working on the enemy," in this case, "the enemy" is the UFO investigator.

Above all, "he learned that penetration of the enemy's intelligence services was crucial in order to nudge the enemy into an unreal world -the famous 'wilderness of mirrors,' that mythical hell to which spy-catchers are consigned by default, doomed to spend their working lives trapped inside the shimmering bars of glancing reflections. It is the place where truth and reality are blinded by deception."

"Counterintelligence has been described as a Dantean hell with ninety-nine circles. Its practitioners are often characterized as tortured souls weltering in an inferno of doubt, half-truths, suspicion, and professional paranoia (1)."

This Dantean hell applies equally well to UFO researchers as it did for those counter-intelligence operatives.

Web links have been utilized as references; we know how links can come and go, but the only other option is have the reader run to the library and get the hard copy reference.

We have focused in on specific personalities and facilities in a very few pages and we hope the references are sufficient. The information on EBEs or Extraterrestrial Biological Entities was group by source. Information that could not be readily verified was placed in the footnotes.

The authors hope the readers will come away from this book having a real appreciation of just how extensive the government's UFO cover-up really is and just how much UFO information remains, "Exempt from Disclosure." — Robert M. Collins, Author: http://www.ufoconspiracy.com/

(1) *Cold Warrior, James Jesus Angleton: The CIA's Master Spy Hunter, 1991,* Touchstone Books, Tom Mangold.

SECTION I: IN THE BEGINNING

Chapter 1

FTD IS NOT A FLORIST!

How did it all get started? After some 20 + years for my contributing writer Rick Doty, and 18 years for me, we still ask that same question considering all the turmoil associated with the subject. As we all know in life, you can 'run into' a subject. Well, one might say I ran into the subject of UFOs while working as an FTD Analyst in the areas of Theoretical & Applied Physics at the Foreign Technology Division (FTD), Wright-Patterson AFB, OH in the summer of 1985. Ever since the end of the Cold War, FTD had undergone several name changes with the latest being the National Air & Space Intelligence Center or NASIC.

Even before being assigned to FTD, like so many others, I had heard all the rumors and stories about alien bodies being stored at Wright-Patterson AFB. Being curious, I started asking many questions, which led me to one Ernie Kellerstrass who had retired from the Air Force in 1979 as a Lieutenant Colonel with FTD being his last Air Force assignment. Ernie was a short pudgy type of person who always seemed to have a menacing, intimidating attitude typical of AF Colonels of the time, yet full of fear and paranoia when talking about UFOs, MJ-12 and aliens, always saying that someone else had told him those stories.

In 1985, Ernie was working for Systems Research Labs located on Indian Ripple Road in Dayton, OH. For someone who was just passing on "stories," he was a treasure trove of information on virtually every aspect of the UFO subject. Ernie mentioned people like Dr. Anthony Joseph Cacioppo (Chief FTD Scientist at the time), Dale Graff (reassigned from FTD to the Defense Intelligence Agency [DIA] now retired) and others as having great in-depth knowledge of the UFO/alien subject. The prime reason according to Ernie, was that both Cacioppo and Graff used to tag along with MJ-12 Team Members to various meetings. One famous meeting was reportedly held at a ski lodge just north of Albuquerque, NM, in 1968 where the topic of concern was a new wave of UFO sightings that made the U.S. government extremely nervous.

Ernie also talked at length about the underground facilities at Wright-Patterson that were reportedly used to house recovered alien artifacts and other facilities nationwide that included the Los Alamos National Labs (LANL) and the National Security Agency or NSA. A good portion of the information that Ernie provided became part of this book.

Go West as they say

In the spring of 1986, I flew out to Los Angeles, California on a TDY (Temporary Duty Assignment for the Air Force) to consult with the technical staff of TRW. While there, I met Bill Moore, who with Charles Berlitz, wrote the first book on Roswell mentioned before (1). Bill came to my motel room where we sat and talked for about an hour. Bill mentioned being contacted in 1980 by a "Mr. X" (see Section 2, Chapter 4, last paragraph in Addendum) who told him at the time that Bill was the only one on the right track among

UFO researchers, so he wanted to work with Bill in a government disclosure process (2). We then both agreed to stay in touch and I returned to Dayton and Wright-Patterson AFB.

So, between what I learned at FTD, and elsewhere, this is how it all began for us as a group. From 1986 onward, Bill Moore, Jaime Shandera (TV producer in North Hollywood, CA), Ernie Kellerstrass (General Dynamics, Wyle Corp, Wright-Patterson AFB; he permanently retired in April 2007), Rick Doty (NM State Trooper), Hal Puthoff (joined the group in 1987, Institute of Advanced Studies in Austin Texas) (3), (4), Dr. Christopher "Kit" Green (joined in 1989 and now at Wayne State Medical Center, Michigan), myself and many others had a succession of meetings dealing with UFOs and the alien subject matter. MJ-12 was often referred to as just the 'Committee' in many of our conversations.

Summits Without the Cocktails, the fall of 1986

Ernie Kellerstrass had Bill Moore, Jaime Shandera, Hal Puthoff, Col. John Alexander (author of the book, *Future War*), Scott Jones (assistant for Senator Pell), and me over to his house in Beavercreek, OH (suburb of Dayton, OH) for dinner. All of our meetings were very somber with most of us looking like stiffs right out of an "X-Files" show. During the dinner and afterwards many of the conversations went non-stop involving such topics as Area 51 in Nevada where purportedly there was an ET base according to Ernie. He also mentioned that on government maps there was an area located northwest of Groom Lake marked "radiation" in which a low yield nuclear device had accidentally detonated many years ago (early to mid '50s). "It's still radioactive, and people were warned to keep out of this specific area. There is supposed to be an ET base in there," Ernie said. It is also an area that the U.S. Government did not want anybody wandering into because anyone who did never returned; they even found security vehicles parked just outside of the area with nobody in them. Kellerstrass said that ostensibly our government never went in there. The idea of an ET base makes you want to stay away, and, of course, you don't know what to make of the stories. So went the conversations in the ensuing months and years until July 1988 when we met again.

And We Became Birds: "The Aviary"

During the interlude, all the players received bird names. Rick Doty was already the surrogate "Falcon" when the real Falcon (DIA's, Dale Graff?) couldn't be found; Ernie became "Hawk," Hal Puthoff became "Partridge," Scott Jones was "Hummingbird," Kit Green became "Blue Jay," John Alexander was "Chickadee" and I, Robert Collins, became "Condor."

August 1988: Cloak & Dagger

Another meeting was to take place in Dayton, OH again, and we all had an elaborate map drawn up by Ernie Kellerstrass showing us how to get to the contact point. Each participant had a different contact point except for the Executive Producer Seligman. Bill Moore, Jaime Shandera and I, were all to meet together. Since we didn't want to cross our signals, and it was important to the executive producer (we felt this was vital to the success of the forthcoming show), Bill and Jaime flew into Dayton OH the night before. I was already in Richmond, IN (40 miles away from Dayton) visiting a friend. The next day we all were able to get local maps and determine how long it would take us to get to the state park. We all traveled separately except for Bill, Jaime and Seligman.

On the way to the contact location, an incredible thunderstorm broke out. It was just pounding. Lucky for us it subsided somewhat so we all made our way down the many roads finally discovering the huge state park. The area had a large lake broken up into a lot of smaller sections with a hilly, wooded area and a large recreation center with a man-made beach.

A couple minutes before 4:00 p.m., the skies began to clear. Bill, Jaime and Seligman (the "UFO Cover-Up Live" producer) got out of the car and began walking toward the beach when all of a sudden, out from a peninsula down to the left came a speedboat. It just came barreling across the lake with a big rooster tail spray behind it. The boat pulled up to the shore and beached then one man jumped off pulling the boat up and called out, "You guys with Bill Moore? We are here for you."

They all walked down toward the boat. Ernie Kellerstrass later said the objective was that we would all be taken in the boat to an island, where there was no communications in or out. No phone lines, no nothing. But, because of the storm, that got a little "iffy" and it was decided that they should take a different tack.

Ernie and his companion turned the boat around and pulled away. Jaime, Bill and Seligman turned around and headed for the car. At that point, I finally pulled up next to their car having traveled separately from Richmond, IN. I followed them and we all headed over to the new location. We assumed that Rick Doty had waited at his assigned location and then left. By the time we got to the other location, everyone had showed up except for Rick Doty. Jaime went to the location where Rick was supposed to be and finding him led him back to where we were.

It turned out that Ernie had somebody with him and, we determined eventually, he was an individual from Air Force's "DET 22." DET 22 is Detachment 22 which is essentially a bodyguard service for anybody in a technical intelligence capacity. Anytime a technician or scientist goes into a foreign country or puts themselves in any other risky travel, they always take a DET 22 person with them (I had a DET 22 person with me when I was on a mission in Germany and France). They are usually fairly knowledgeable about the subject at hand, but their principal function is escort. The very strange thing about Ernie having a DET 22 person with him was that he had been retired from the Air Force since 1979 and was working for SRL, so why the DET 22 person? To this day we have no answer for that question.

All our discussions were very frank and straightforward. Credentials were shown, the executive producer wanted to look at our picture ID CARDS so that he could be 100 percent certain of the sources and their specific functions and agencies they belonged to. He also elicited their cooperation by allowing him to run a background check. He eventually hired a Congressional Investigator to determine if these men were indeed bona fide agents within the agencies they had claimed affiliations with. They all checked out. The discussions were informative. There was some new information, and some old information that all of us were familiar with; no tape recorders or cameras were allowed.

Even amongst fellow spooks there was a cat and mouse game going during the meeting. Rick and Ernie ostensibly had not met before, and they were doing a little challenging back and forth as to who knew what. One would start to describe a certain classified room in the Pentagon or something, and then say, "Oh yeah, and then when you go through this door...um what was it again on the other side of that wall?" If the other spook could pick up the conversation from there and describe it, and everybody was in sync, then everything continued along. At the same time, they began talking about the ET who was an "ambassador" or liaison to the U.S. Among the things discussed was that the extraterrestrial ambassador was a female, Extraterrestrial Biological Entity (EBE-3?) or some other female EBE? We really didn't know the answer to that. See Section 2, Chapter 4.

The extraterrestrials supposedly had a book known as the "Yellow Book." The Yellow Book was a history of the extraterrestrials written by them. There was talk about a crystal that when an ET held it and turned it in certain ways, it showed pictures of their home planet, and what life was like on that planet. Agent Rick Doty indicated that he had seen that crystal, and in fact had handled it, but couldn't make it work. It seemed to work only when an ET handled it. We all had a fascinating discussion; quite an earful was learned by Seligman and some of the others. Further arrangements for additional contacts were set up and at the end of the meeting we parted company with all the participants heading in separate directions. Once Bill and Jaime got back to Los Angeles, they started putting together all of the material that had been gathered during all the meetings including the most recent one. The biggest obstacle was how to make use of the information and dig out

further information for use in the upcoming October 1988 show.
Seligman, Rick and I all headed back to California and New Mexico
respectively. I was stationed at Kirtland AFB, Air Force Weapons
Lab at the time.

September 1988

Interviews were needed for the upcoming October 1988 UFO show. We all
met in Albuquerque, NM, where Bill and Jaime shot an interview with the
surrogate Falcon (Rick Doty), and they also shot an interview with me
(Condor). They also shot an interview with Richard Doty as just 'Special OSI
Agent' Rick Doty who was just leaving the Air Force. Ultimately, Rick's
unmasked interview did not make it to the "UFO Cover-Up Live" show
since all of the interviews were running over their time limit. The show
finally aired on October 14, 1988 and, as we found out later, the
phones were burning off the hook in Washington D.C. Almost
immediately, Bill and Jaime had two new high-level contacts who
had approached them. They were aware of these individuals before
and introductions were immediately arranged. There were now two
new birds in the Aviary.

April 1989

Time for another mini-summit and this time around there was
absolutely no reason to involve the executive producer Seligman.
The meeting was held in Albuquerque, NM, at a motel. We had
Partridge (Hal Puthoff), Blue Jay (Kit Green), Rick Doty, Bill and
Jaime and me at this mini-summit. This meeting dealt with the after
shocks from the "UFO Cover-Up Live" show and how to proceed
with the new sources. Kit Green took center stage by proposing
several lines of attack involving disclosure strategies.

In the next few years after 1988 and '89, relationships with
several new contacts developed. An old contact friend, Richard
Helms (ex-CIA Director) was renamed Mr. R. (in 1991) by Rick
Doty and sometimes called "Raven," but not to be confused with
Jaime Shandera's "Raven," with more on that later. Then in 1995,

Jaime had a fateful meeting with our "Mr. X" near the mall in Washington D.C. see Section 2 Chapter 4. All of these meetings and contacts of course were handled in the utmost covert manner.

To this day many of us still stay in contact (except for Bill & Jaime) coordinating information while talking with our sources. All of the sources were used in one way or another as a basis for this book. So, what is MJ-12 and how does it relate to everything else and the cover-up? Chapter 2 and later in Section 2, we will attempt to address those important questions.

References/Footnotes

(1) *The Roswell Incident*, Charles Berlitz & William L. Moore, 1980 G.P. Putnam's Sons, 1988 Berkley Publishing Group.

(2) Rick Doty said on February 21, 2005, "Bill Moore had several sources within the U.S. Government, one being a "Mr. X," as he called the source. I have no idea who this source was or what this source's connection was with the government. Moore never disclosed his sources. According to Linda Howe, Moore had sources within NSA, CIA, DIA and FBI. I never met Moore with anyone other than official personnel. On one occasion, I met Moore with an NSA investigator, but most of the officials were OSI agents. During the Bennewitz affair, I met Moore with FBI agents."

(3) H.E. Puthoff, J. Deardorff, B. Haisch, and B. Maccabee, "Inflation-Theory: Implications for Extraterrestrial Visitation," JBIS, Vol. 58, pp 43-50, 2005, http://www.ufoskeptic.org/JBIS.pdf.

(4) Selected Institute for Advanced Studies and EarthTech International Publications, http://earthtech.org/publications/.

Chapter 2

WHAT IS MJ-12?

There are numerous books and Web sites devoted to this subject, so we shall only visit briefly on the subject then move to some of the key players who played significant, historically important roles related to this group.

Operation Majestic-12 was established by a special classified presidential order on September 24, 1947 at the recommendation of Secretary of Defense James Forrestal and Dr. Vannevar Bush, Chairman of the Joint Research and Development Board. The goal of the group was to exploit everything they could from recovered alien technology (1-3).

As a brief aside: Interestingly enough, the "OROCA Panel" was reportedly to be even higher than MJ-12 (see "Quoth the Raven," Section 2, Chapter 4 Addendum). In the '80s, MJ-12 was hidden away at the NSA in the "C Group." In 1986 it became the "Special Advisory Group-12." Then in Circa 2000, MJ-12's new designation reportedly became, the "Counsel of 12, Special Security Alliance" with new caveats of SIMCO (Special Intra-military Cooperation Office), and TIOP (Technical Information Operations Panel) which replaced the caveat MAJIC. Name changing is the favorite pass time of the bean counters.

Ambitious, elite scientists such as Vannevar Bush, Albert Einstein, and Robert Oppenheimer, and career military people such as Hoyt Vandenberg, Roscoe Hillenkoetter, Leslie Groves, and George Marshall, along with a select cast of other experts (MJ-12 Support Team Members), had feverishly and secretively labored to understand the alien agenda, technology and its implications for our own technology (see (1) and for additional MJ-12 Support Team Members see footnotes 2 and 3).

Einstein and Oppenheimer were called in to give their opinions, drafting a six-page paper titled "Relationships with Inhabitants of Celestial Bodies." They provided prophetic insight into our modern nuclear strategies and satellites, and expressed agitated urgency that an agreement should be reached with the president so that scientists could proceed to study the alien technology.

The extraordinary recovery of fallen airborne objects in the state of New Mexico, between July 4 and July 6, 1947, had caused the Chief of Staff of the Army Air Force's Interplanetary Phenomena Unit (IPU), Scientific and Technical Branch, Counterintelligence Directorate to initiate a thorough investigation. From what has been learned recently, that special unit was formed in 1942 in response to two (2) crashes in the Los Angeles area in late February 1942 (1). The draft summary report begins: "At 2332 MST, 3 July 47, radar stations in east Texas and White Sands Proving Ground, N.M. tracked two unidentified aircraft until they both dropped off the radar. Two crash sites have been located close to the WSPG. Site LZ-1 was located at a ranch near Corona, approx. 75 miles northwest of the town of Roswell. Site LZ-2 was located approximately 20 miles southeast of the town of Socorro, at latitude 33-40-31 and longitude 106-28-29."

The crash near Corona is said to be detailed in an official Defense Intelligence Agency [DIA] "Digest" called the "Red Book." But, the crash at LZ-2 is not. Instead the "Digest" lists a crash west of Socorro in 1947 that wasn't recovered until 1948 or '49.

The first-ever-known UFO crash retrieval case was to have occurred in 1941 at Cape Girardeau, MO. This crash kicked off early reverse-engineering work, but it did not create a unified intelligence effort to exploit possible technological gains apart from the Manhattan Project uses.

The debris from the primary field of the 1947 crash 20 miles southeast of Socorro, NM, was called ULAT-1 (Unidentified Lenticular Aerodyne Technology), and it excited metallurgists with its unheard of tensile and shear strengths. The nuclear process (called neutronic at that time) engine used heavy water and deuterium with an oddly arranged series of coils, magnets, and electrodes — descriptions that resemble the "cold fusion" studies of today. But, this setup could have also been related to the use of the isotope H5 (see LANL Reverse Engineering in Section 3, Chapter 3).

Harry Truman kept the technical briefing documents of September 24, 1947, for further study, pondering the challenges of creating and funding a secret organization before the CIA existed (although the Central Intelligence Group or CIG did exist) and before there was a legal procedure for funding non-war operations.

In April 1954, a group of senior officers of the U.S. intelligence community and the Armed Forces gathered for one of the most secret and sensational briefings in history. The subject was Unidentified Flying Objects — not just a discussion of sightings, but how to recover crashed UFOs, where to ship the parts, and how to deal with the occupants (Ed Doty, the uncle of Rick Doty informed these authors that he attended a "UFO Crash Recovery" course at LANL in 1954). For example, in the "Special Operations Manual (SOM1-01) Extraterrestrial Entities Technology Recovery and Disposal," MAJESTIC–12 "Red Teams" mapped out UFO crash retrieval scenarios with special attention given to press blackouts, their body packaging, live alien transport, isolation, and custody.

UFO-related secret programs have consumed a significant part of America's "black budget" since the Manhattan Project. For example, the 1997 government-disclosed intelligence budget portion alone was $26 billion and according to Tim Weiner's 1990 book, *Blank Check*, the total black-budget was about $35 billion. Even the most sensational conspiracy of modern times—the Kennedy assassination—could likely be linked to the UFO cover-up and the military cabal, as several of the documents seem to demonstrate (see reference (1) and Chapters 1 and 2 in Section 2).

Overall, the United States UFO program grew out of necessity. First, to determine the alien threat; second, to exploit their advanced technology in anyway we could to gain a military, economic or even a psychological advantage and win World War II; and third, to maintain power, authority, control of technology, governments, and world stability. Initially, to make the project public would have sent unpredictable turmoil into science, religion, politics, and global economics. But beyond those reasons, was religious and political power the overriding reason for the suppression of extraterrestrial knowledge with religion of the greatest concern? (See footnote 4). Governments and religious authorities have a long history of suppressing knowledge that conflict with traditional beliefs, so who were some of the players involved in this conspiracy? What roles had James Jesus Angleton, Allen Dulles, Richard Helms, Rick Doty and those mysterious Men-in-Black played in the cover-up? Section 2 will attempt to answers those questions and more.

References/Footnotes

(1) For MJ-12 documents and reports see, http://www.majesticdocuments.com/.

(2) The following are photos of supposed MJ-12 Support Team Members from a confidential LANL source. Most of these team members still remain unidentified despite intense concerted efforts to identify them.

Figure 1: Counting from left to right at bottom in sitting position; Theodore von Karman is third from left with his left arm resting on a chair. In the next to the very back left of middle standing straight up and wearing glasses is Leonard Wendling (Dayton Ohio) of the Navy. Others remain unidentified. Von Karman's name can be found throughout many of the MJ-12 documents; see Majestic personnel and then documents at: http://www.majesticdocuments.com.

Figure 2*:* MJ-12 Team members at LANL circa 1958 with 7 members of the new MJ-12 team received from the confidential LANL source with no details. Major General Whitehead is center in above photo and on extreme right in Figure 3 photo. The only person that could be identified in this photo was of Whitehead. Who was Whitehead?

Figure 3: Major General Ennis R. Whitehead is on the extreme right in this photo with Douglas McArthur in the center. Picture taken in the Southwest Pacific during one of McArthur's visits to the American troops who immediately afterward made their first landing on New Britain, a major Japanese base during WW II. Other people identified left to right: Major General S. J. Chamberlin, General MacArthur's Operations Officer, Lt. General Walter Kreueger, Commander of the American Sixth Army; Brig. General E. D. Patrick, Chief of Staff of the Sixth Army; Vice-Admiral Thomas C. Kinkaid, Commander of the Allied Naval Forces. Chamberlin later rose to become the Assistant Chief of Staff, G-2 (Intelligence) in the summer of 1947 and was one of the members of the summer

"Mission" resulting in the report on recovered lenticular aerodyne objects of September 1947 see, http://209.132.68.98/pdf/twining_whitehotreport.pdf.

Figure 4: MJ-12 Team members at Holloman AFB NM, April 1964?

Received from the confidential LAN source, but this picture was not taken in 1964. From the evidence it seems this was taken in either late 1945 or early1946 perhaps at Los Alamos. The aircraft in the background is a C97 cargo/refueling aircraft. Robert Oppenheimer is on the extreme left. Nathan Twining of MJ-12 fame is on the extreme right. Edward Condon of the famous University of Colorado Condon Report on UFOs is next to Twining. Both Oppenheimer and Condon were Nuclear Physicist. Neither of the other two gentlemen can be identified. Oppenheimer and Twining's names can be found in a number of MJ-12 documents with one entitled, Twining's "White Hot Report: Mission Assessment of Recovered Lenticular Aerodyne Objects," see: http://209.132.68.98/pdf/twining_whitehotreport.pdf.

**MJ-12 Reunion
Los Alamos National Laboratory
August 16-17, 2003
Starlight Teams, Victor and Sierra**

Figure 5: MJ-12 team reunion, Los Alamos National Laboratory, August 10-17, 2003: Starlight Team Victor and Sierra. Figure 5 is another mysterious photo supposedly representing an MJ-12 team reunion at Los Alamos in August 2003. Like with other MJ-12 team photos, our research and best efforts have not revealed who most of these people are. Since government counter-intelligence does such a good job of concealing the records of these MJ-12 team members, research becomes extremely difficult if not impossible.

(3) MJ-12 Organizational Support list: Late '40s to mid-'90s

The first reported lists of individuals who were connected to the original MJ-12 team: Part of the reported MJ-12 Group Technical Advisory Panel (MTAP-12), see document in reference 5 (Figure 6).

a) Arthur Lundahl: CIA 1953-1974, founder and director of the CIA's Photographic Interpretation Center, he discovered Russian missiles in Cuba and briefed three presidents on UFOs.

b) Stanley Schneider: Former assistant to the director, White House Office of Science and Technology.

c) Lt Col Robert Friend: USAF: Commanding Officer, Project Blue Book, 1958-1963.

d) Dr. Charles Sheldon: head of Science and Technology Division, Library of Congress, U.S Office of Naval Intelligence and former CIA employee.

e) Arnold White: Chief, CIA Domestic Contact Division, 1952-1973.

f) Dr. Gerald Rothberg: Stevens Institute of Technology: Served on the Condon Committee: CIA Team Chief on operation "Christopher Columbus."

g) General James Garland, USAF: Former commanding officer, ATIC.

h) General William Hipps, USAF: Former commander USAF Intelligence Operations Command ('50s).

This second list is reported to be individuals who were on the MJ-12 Group Technical Advisory Panel (MTAP-12) from the early 1950s until the late '60s.

a) Louis A. Johnson: served from March 28, 1949 to September 19, 1950, second Secretary of Defense, Truman Administration.

b) Harold C. Stuart: no information found.

c) John C. McCone: Director of Central Intelligence, 29 November 1961–28 April 1965

d) Thomas K. Finletter: 1893-1980, consultant to United States delegation to the United Nations Conference on International Organization, San Francisco, May 1945; Chairman, President's Air Policy Commission, 1947-1948. He was minister in charge of the Economic Cooperation. He was on an administration mission to the United Kingdom, 1948-1949 and Secretary of the Air Force, 1950-1953.

e) General Earle Partridge 1900-1990: in April 1954, as a four-star general, he became commander of the Far East Air Forces in Tokyo. Partridge returned home in July 1955 and was named commander in chief of the North American Air Defense Command and its Air Force

Component, the Air Defense Command at ENT Air Force Base, Colorado Springs. He retired from active duty on July 31, 1959.

f) Dr. John Von Neumann: born in 1903, Budapest, Hungary; died 8 February 1957, Washington DC; brilliant mathematician, synthesizer, and promoter of the stored program concept, whose logical design of the IAS became the prototype of most of its successors, " the von Neumann Architecture."

g) Eger V. Murphree, 1898-1962: former president of Exxon Research & Engineering Co. (ER&E); was one of four Exxon inventors who created the fluid catalytic cracking process. When ER & E's's first commercial cat cracking facility went on-line in 1942, the U.S. had just entered World War II and was facing a shortage of high-octane aviation gasoline.

Most recent individuals reportedly involved in the MJ-12 program. Note: MJ-12 was reportedly re-designated the Special Advisory Group-12 in 1986, no further information is available.

a) Richard Helms: Director of Central Intelligence, 30 June 1966- 2 February 1973, see Section 2, Chapter 3.

b) William Colby: Director of Central Intelligence, 4 September 1973 – 30 January 1976.

c) Lou Tordella: 1911-1996: became the deputy director of the NSA in 1958, and remained in the post until his retirement in 1974, and was the longest serving deputy director in the NSA's history.

d) John Tovey: we are not sure who this person was nor what position he held.

e) Senator Pell: a Democrat of Newport, Rhode Island, he was born in New York City on November 22, 1918. He served as United States Senator from Rhode Island, 1961-1997.

f) Dr. Carl Sagan, 1934-1996: Carl Sagan published more than 600 scientific papers and popular articles and is author, co-author or editor of more than 20 books, including *The Dragons of Eden* (1977), for which he won the Pulitzer Prize in 1978. The U.S. paperbound edition of his book

Pale Blue Dot: A Vision of the Human Future in Space appeared on best-seller lists worldwide and was selected as one of the " most notable books of 1995" by The New York Times.

g) Ken Shutten: no information found.

h) Dr. Raemer Schreiber, between 1948-1955, he was successively Associate Leader and Leader of the division charged with weapons engineering at Los Alamos. In 1955, he became leader of the division charged with the assembly of reactors for rocket propulsion, and in 1962 he was made Technical Associate Director of the Los Alamos Scientific Laboratory, with direct responsibility for the whole program for the development of nuclear propulsion for rockets and space vehicles.

(4) Tim Cooper in 2000 writes: In the spring of 1947, in a small cave overlooking the Dead Sea in Palestine, a 15-year-old boy stood in the dim light and stared bewilderedly at a mass of leather wrapped in a linen cloth. The unsightly bundle was stored in a large, two-foot-high clay pot.

This lad held in his hands what has since been termed "the greatest manuscript discovery of modern times. ... an absolutely incredible find!" Here were parts of the Bible that date back into the second century B.C.E. (Before the Common Era), over 1000 years earlier than the oldest copies available up to that time. How would they compare with the more recent copies? Millar Burrows, who worked with the scrolls for years carefully analyzing their contents, stated there was "a remarkable agreement, on the whole, with the text found in medieval manuscripts." The differences were so slight and negligible that it gave "reassuring testimony to the general accuracy of the traditional text." Burrows further exclaimed, "It is a matter for wonder that through something like a thousand years the text underwent so little alteration."

A textual discovery of another kind reportedly occurred some years later in the New Mexican desert by U.S. military authorities.

Harry Cooper (my father), a retired AF MSgt (1963) who died in September 2000, said that a very ancient Hebrew bible, written in a Hebrew language predating anything so far discovered, was recovered from a large ovul object buried in the sand. The recovery team had no idea how long the object had been there. This incident reportedly occurred near White

Sands in March 1947. James Jesus Angleton was there, see Chapter 1 in Section II). A Colonel Paul Helmick who was then commander of Alamogordo Army Airfield (later to become Holloman AFB) ordered Harry Cooper (then NCOIC of the Photo Lab) to print up a report on the White Sands oval object recovery. Part of that report referenced the recovered ancient Hebrew bible; reportedly, the report was forwarded to Col Helmick and then onto Wright Field (a).

Just after this March 1947 NM incident, a liaison was established with a Hebrew language scholar (we believe it was William F. Albright, a well known Biblical scholar and the father of modern Biblical archaeology) for a textual comparison between the Dead Sea Scrolls and what was found in what can only be described as a space craft of unknown origin. This incident was depicted in both an episode of the "X-Files" and a Discovery Channel program which covered the "Bible Code." However, these depictions did not directly address the story given in the preceding paragraphs (see, reference b for further information).

Comment from Robert Collins: Could there be a simpler explanation as to why this ancient Hebrew Bible was found in this particular UFO? Can we assume that all space-venturing beings love souvenirs and that they have been souvenir hunting on this planet for over 10,000 years according to Extraterrestrial Biological Entity-1 (EBE-1)? Is it possible they brought this ancient Hebrew Bible with them in circa 1947 as a reference, but why? Was it for the purpose of creating crop circles with ancient Hebrew symbols like those crop circles with Sumerian symbols?

As the story is told, in 1955, senior code breakers at the U.S. National Security Agency (NSA) (see reference 5, Figure 6 for Alien Codex also done by NSA) completed deciphering this "Hebrew" Bible code; that information was transmitted to the infamous secret government UFO investigative group known as MJ-12. According to certain sources (one was Cantwheel) who leaked MJ-12 documents in the 1990s, "The Hebrew Bible was confirmed as the long sought after key to understanding extraterrestrial UFO sightings ... and this information was shared with the Vatican as early as 1949." As incredible as this might sound, it must be remembered that the Air Force's Project SIGN staff had considered Biblical UFO sightings and the writings of Charles Fort in its attempt to put a historical label on flying saucer reports prior to the 20th century. But, since this particular story only has a few sources, it will have to sit in the hearsay column or, "grey basket" for now (b).

(a) Tim Cooper contacted Paul Helmick by phone a few years ago. As Tim recounts Helmick was livid when asked about the 1947 Alamogordo UFO recovery in the sand and his relationship with Tim's father, Harry Cooper. Helmick was reassigned from Alamogordo to Edwards AFB retiring in the years 1953-54.

(b) Tim Cooper writes on July 13, 2000: "I might have over stepped literary license a little. This is what Cantwheel told me verbally in 1995 and by another source whom I knew in 1990. Cantwheel said that military and civilian intelligence contacted William F. Albright at Johns Hopkins to examine selected scripts they had found for comparison to the photographed Dead Sea Scrolls that he looked at in 1947. Albright died in 1971 and I have not gotten independent confirmation as of yet. I have been told that William Friedman and Callahamos at NSA completed the linguistic analysis sometime in 1954-1955 and that Einstein was consulted on some cosmological aspects of it before he died in 1955. From what I understand, Albright commented that the New Mexico script was written in a proto-Hebrew language deemed much older than the Hebrew Moses might have used to compile Genesis."

(5) See next page for Figure 6: comments about Figure 6. This document has received confirmation from two separate sources which support the fact that there was an EXCOM (Executive Committee; setup to deal with the Cuban missile crisis) meeting at the time/date specified in the Project Jehovah MJ-12 document on page 26. One source is, "An Unfinished Life" (a book about JFK's life, 2003) pages 559-65 and the other source is a FOIA document released in 1988, see link below. This document also confirms that a Dr. Weisner (MIT Science Adviser to JFK) was present at the meeting.
http://www.gwu.edu/~nsarchiv/nsa/publications/cmc/cmcdoc2.html

CODE WORD WHITE PEBBLE
MAJCOMSEC INTELLIGENCE EYES ONLY

PROJECT JEHOVAH

SUBJECT: NATIONAL SECUIRTY AGENCY CODE BREAKING OF ALIEN
CODEX AND HISTORICAL RESEARCH OF THE CENTRAL INTELLIGENCE
AGENCY'S MJEBEN PROGRAM AND DEPARTMENT OF DEFENSE U.F.O.
IDENTIFICATION AND DETECTION PROJECT FIRESTONE.

PREPARED BY: MJ-12 GROUP TECHNICAL ADVISORY PANEL (MTAP-12)

FOR USE BY: EMERGENCY COMBAT COMMUNICATIONS (ECOMCOM)

COMPLETED ON: OCTOBER 2, 1962

APPROVED BY: EXECUTIVE COMMITTEE (EXCOM) ON OCTOBER 24,
1962, 10:00 A.M., MEETING NO. 3

NOTE: This document is based on NSA and CIA COMINT files and the USAF
Project BLUE BOOK and Special Reports 1-14. Dr. Wiesner presented an initial
briefing on the ECOMCOM situation and the President directed that most urgent
action be taken by State, Defense and CIA to improve communications worldwide.

EXECUTIVE BRIEFING DOCUMENT
DO NOT REMOVE FROM VAULT ROOM
MAJESTIC TWELVE CLEARANCE REQUIRED
WARNING!
THIS IS AN EXECUTIVE BRIEFING DOCUMENT, CONTAINING
SENSITIVE INTELLIGENCE INFORMATION WHOSE DISCLOSURE
TO UNAUTHORIZED PERSONS CONSTITUTES A SERIOUS
BREACH OF NATIONAL SECURITY. DISSEMINATION OR
REPRODUCTION IN ANY MANNER IS STRICTLY FORBIDDEN.
ANY VIOLATIONS OF THIS CAVEAT IS PUNISHABLE UNDER THE
CENTRAL INTELLIGENCE AGENCY ACT, ANY OR ALL
APPLICABLE FEDERAL ESPIONAGE LAWS AND NATIONAL
SECUIRTY ACTS AS AMENDED.

Figure 6: Bleed through cover page copy of 1962 MJ-12
Exective Briefing for JFK.

SECTION II: PLAYERS

JAMES JESUS ANGLETON JJA, DIRECTOR OF COUNTER-INTELLIGENCE (DD/CI) AND GURADIAN OF THE CIA's GREATEST SECRET

James Jesus Angleton was born on 9 December 1917, in Boise, Idaho, to NCR businessman Colonel James Hugh Angleton (a member OSS in WWII or, Office of Strategic Services, predecessor to the CIA), and Mexican born Carmen Mercedes Moreno. Upon graduation from Yale in 1941, Angleton moved to Harvard Law School where he met his future wife Cicely d'Autremont of Duluth, MN. Inducted into the U.S. Army on 19 March 1943, Angleton was recruited into the OSS in August through the efforts of Angleton's father and Norman Pearson, his old English professor from Yale who was, at that time, head of the OSS Counter Intelligence division in London (1).

Angleton as CIA Agent in OSS X-2 Operations During WWII

James Angleton was assigned the Rome desk after Italy's capitulation to the Allies and was made an OSS Lieutenant who ran CI activities that included such countries as Austria, Germany, Spain, the Mediterranean, and Switzerland. As part of OSS operations in the European Theatre of Operations, Angleton mastered the art of "black" propaganda and "playback," i.e., the method of reading the effectiveness of one's own disinformation on the enemy. In 1944, he was given charge of the OSS Special Counterintelligence Unit Z made up of U.S. and British agents and was the youngest member of X-2 and the only American member that was allowed access to the top secret British ULTRA code breaking intelligence. After the war, Angleton was promoted to captain and received the Legion of Merit award from the U.S. Army, which cited him for successfully apprehending over a thousand enemy intelligence agents. He was also decorated by the Italian government and was awarded the Order of the Crown of Italy, the Order of Malta-Cross of Malta, and the Italian War Cross for Merit. In October 1945, President Truman dissolved the OSS, and had all the research, analysis units moved to the State Department and operational units to the War Department. The OSS was re-named the Strategic Services Unit (SSU). Angleton stayed on in the SSU in Rome and became the vital station chief in charge of the 2677th Regiment. They made Angleton the senior U.S. intelligence officer in Italy until it became the Central Intelligence Group, forerunner of the Central Intelligence Agency (2).

The Making of James Angleton as Master Spy Hunter

Angleton's war experience in counterintelligence operations had affected him to the extent that he became absorbed into the 'hall of mirrors' world of intelligence and refused to leave despite the insistence and disappointment of his father. James would pour over the many CI files he amassed while in Italy and was forever changed by the intrigue and the possibilities of a career in the CIG. In the summer of 1947, he returned to the United States to live in Tucson, AZ with his wife and family, but his love for the service was overpowering and, on 30 December 1947, he was hired by the CIA as a senior aide to the director of the Office of Special Operations (OSO) (3). It was during this period that Army G-2 and other intelligence agencies were trying to crack the Soviet VENONA code used by espionage agents operating in the United States. These agents were sending back sensitive information regarding the Manhattan Project based at Los Alamos, NM. It is possible that Angleton was on special assignment prior to officially reporting to OSO who had the responsibility of running counterespionage operations (4).

His primary mission in OSO included overseeing a classified component that operated espionage and counterespionage activities abroad. He read all the sensitive material coming across his desk and then passed them back to OSO operators in countries where the CIA had interests. In 1949, Angleton had moved up the chain of command within OSO and held a GS-15 position. Angleton developed a philosophy that, "If you control counterintelligence, you control the intelligence service," and quickly realized the significance of the B-29 detection of Joe-1, the Soviet's first atomic weapon detonation in August 1949. Angleton knew the technology required by the Soviets was not home grown, but rather the product of espionage and he immediately set out to discover who the moles were that passed on America's most guarded secret to Moscow. As with all covert actions, counterintelligence operated without specific mentioning in the National Security Act of 1947 which gave Angleton the excuse he needed to pursue information on the most guarded of all secrets.

James Angleton as Deputy Director for Counterintelligence (DD/CI)

Aside from the technology theft of atomic secrets, one of the most guarded secrets within the CIA was the scientific and technical information regarding new weapons developments and the planned use of a new generation of Thermal Nuclear Weapons and high altitude reconnaissance platforms to spy on countries hostile to United States strategic interests. One of the technical secrets of the United States was the study and transfer of advanced electronics gleaned from Air Force studies of unconventional aircraft and missile research carried on at several Atomic Energy Commission (AEC) facilities and proving grounds. The FBI and the CIA were aware of Soviet espionage rings operating in the United States, Canada and the United Kingdom. The espionage ring's main task was providing any and all technical and scientific information on advanced technologies which could provide an advantage to the Soviet Union in the event of another world war.

By 1949, military intelligence authorities had classified the "flying saucer" phenomenon as "Top Secret" and Army's Counter-intelligence Corps (CIC) had passed on information that the Soviets may have developed saucer-shaped aerial weapons capable of delivering atomic bombs or dissipating radioactive materials over NATO countries as a stop-gap measure to make up for the nonexistent nuclear weapons arsenal. In early 1947, the nonexistent nuclear arsenal in the United States was a closely guarded secret and no doubt this fact set in motion the nuclear arms race which terrified Angleton. OSO was probably aware of Soviet knowledge of a bomb gap existing within both superpowers and the flying saucer invasion of the United States which crossed Angleton's desk. This put a scare into his psyche reflected as a credo he shared with other OSO staff members: "You who believe or half believe, I can say this now, that I do believe in the spirit of Christ and the life everlasting, and in this turbulent social system which struggles sometimes blindly to preserve the right to freedom and expression of spirit. In the name of Jesus Christ, I leave you."

After General Walter B. Smith was appointed as Director of Central Intelligence (DCI), Angleton continued on as OSO Staff "A" (foreign intelligence operations) inside the CIA's clandestine division. In 1951, he was given the all-important Israeli desk which he held tight control over for 20 years because it was a source of vital Soviet information in the Middle East as more and more UFO sighting reports made their way to CIA headquarters (5) (also see WBS memos in Chapter 3, Figures 2 and 3). Raw, unevaluated reports were forwarded to counterintelligence when the locations were identified as Soviet bloc countries. During this period, Angleton made good liaisons with FBI contacts who were equally concerned with protecting vital atomic research facilities and no doubt Angleton read many domestic reports as they came across his desk in the "L" Building across from the Lincoln Memorial. When Smith was coaxed away from his power base as DCI, Allen Dulles, Angleton's friend from the OSS days, became the new DCI. In late 1954, he promoted Angleton to the position of deputy director and Chief of Counterintelligence. Angleton had direct access to Dulles and all foreign UFO intelligence from the Intelligence Advisory Committee which had been established to look into national security implications involving the UFO phenomena (6). In order to cement Angleton's counterintelligence charter together, General James H. Doolittle was commissioned by Dulles to conduct an outside survey of CIA counterintelligence operations. He concluded that the CIA was losing ground to the KGB and recommended more stringent and ruthless measures be taken against Soviet penetration. Dulles endorsed the Doolittle Report by ordering a more powerful tool to stop and interdict the moles within the CIA, and he personally chose Angleton to head the CI staff. Perhaps this is why foreign and domestic UFO sighting reports diminished shortly thereafter.

During Dulles' tenure as DCI from 1953 to 1961 (next Chapter, longest in CIA history), Angleton enjoyed a privileged position (as he did with other future DCIs like McCone and Helms Chapter 3) not shared by other directors despite the fact that he reported to the Deputy Director of

Operations [DDO]. On many occasions, he bugged the phones and residences of high ranking U.S. government officials and foreign dignitaries with Dulles' approval and over the objection of the DDO. If the situation called for it, Angleton could go around proper channels for acquiring personal data on anyone within the CIA and other agencies which was clearly outside of the CIA charter and violated FBI jurisdiction. As the new head of CI, he had to organize a staff, write the rules, and oversee all clandestine operations aimed at Soviet military and security organs of the GRU and KGB (7). The CI staff was primarily tasked with preventing penetrations at home and abroad and protecting CIA operations through careful research and analysis of all incoming intelligence reports. By keeping the most vital and sensitive files to himself, Angleton became a storehouse of secrets, which helped him consolidate his power base. Officially, Angleton was allowed access to everyone's personnel, operational, and communications files within the CIA. He reviewed all proposed and active operations and the approval for recruiting agent assets. This did not engender trust or cooperation, but Angleton did not concern himself as he felt the intrusions were needed. One of Angleton's former Chief of Operations, "Scotty" Miller, expressed the environment in which CI staff operated as one of a "watchdog" snooping around to sniff out either Soviet deception or manipulation.

Angleton and the MJ-12 Directive

Cold War hysteria that accompanied the "duck and cover" scare that seemed to grip the nation. No real problems popped up until the 1960 presidential elections when Democratic presidential candidate Senator John F. Kennedy accused the Republican incumbent President Eisenhower of allowing a "missile gap" to exist and charged that the United States was getting too close to the Soviet Union.

Soon after Kennedy became president, he began to needle the CIA for information on UFOs (11) which was unnerving from the outset for Allen Dulles after he was just burned on the failed April 1961 Bay of Pigs invasion of communist-enslaved Cuba. The once cordial relationship that had existed fell apart and Dulles knew his time as DCI was short (12). Dulles knew of the explicit instructions contained in the 24 September 1947 Truman directive; it prohibits the DCI from making disclosures to a chief executive who obviously did not have a "need-to-know." Disclosure without a "need-to-know" might not only compromise the CIA, but the lengthy and costly UFO program deemed so necessary to national security by all involved. This simply could not be jeopardized for any one person, even for the president of the United States. Knowing the character of Allen Dulles and James Angleton, we can only speculate as to what kind of response Kennedy may have received. According to the DCI Top Secret/MJ-12 document, it leaves no doubt that Dulles was not going to fully cooperate with Kennedy's request, but instead forwarded it to Angleton for review, consideration and feedback. MJ MAJESTIC TWELVE included spin-off projects that were obviously equally sensitive activities of the CIA such as PARASITE, PARHELION, ENVIRO, PSYOP, GREEN, SPIKE, and HOUSE CLEANING. Other sensitive and covert programs could be affected as well, such as MK ULTRA, ARTICHOKE and DOMESTIC all of which appear to have been valid projects associated with MJ MAJESTIC TWELVE. The full implications of the above are not clear at the present time, but it is obvious that the other projects were held in readiness for some kind of mass indoctrination and deception which would be undertaken in a national crisis.

Murder, INC.

The strain mounted on the CIA by Kennedy was reaching a flash point of wills and with the Noresenko affair (13) driving Angleton to obsession, a UFO leak crisis brought new strains on Angleton. He had learned of Hollywood screen star Marilyn Monroe's phone conversation with a New York art dealer (14) discussing Kennedy's secret visit to an undisclosed military base to see alien artifacts (this could have been Ft. Belvoir, Annex K or Wright-Patterson AFB). With that was her disdain over the soured relationship she had endured with President Kennedy and his brother, the United States Attorney General, Robert F. Kennedy, all of which had been recorded by CIA domestic electronic surveillance experts. Since 1955, Monroe had been under surveillance by the CIA and the FBI. They had maintained a security dossier on her because of her marriage with a well-known American writer who was suspected of having communist affiliations. They also tracked her trip to Russia and the press coverage she received while there (15). The wiretap report also mentions nationally recognized New York syndicated reporter Dorothy Kilgallen as having conversations with Monroe regarding the Roswell UFO crash of 1947 and President Kennedy's politically motivated NASA Apollo moon program. Dorothy Kilgallen also made headlines in 1955 when she disclosed a private conversation with a British cabinet official that UFOs were real and that the U.S. and British authorities considered the matter of the highest national importance. The significance of the wiretap was that Monroe was murdered the following day in her Brentwood condo. According to internationally recognized private investigator and director of the Nick Harris Detective Agency, Milo Speriglio. Monroe was the victim of a national security management hit by the CIA and the MAFIA (16). The suggestion that somehow the CIA was involved in a domestic murder of an American citizen is not too far fetched when considering the past abuses coming from Angleton's CI program of 'absolute-security-at-any-cost' philosophy. Whether Angleton authorized the hit is not known, but the modus operandi of the way her body was found and moved around and the fashion in which the autopsy records were changed to reflect suicide plus the theft of her secret red diary one day after her autopsy is similar to the past methods used by Angleton's covert CIA counterintelligence operators.

Active Measures

The final straw for Angleton came when President Kennedy fired off a top-secret memorandum to him outlining a previous discussion concerning a classification review of all CIA UFO files that could affect national security. It was dated 12 November 1963, just 10 days before he would be gunned down on the streets of Dallas, TX. Kennedy informed Angleton (17) that he was setting things in motion to actually share sensitive CIA UFO intelligence data with the Russians through the director of NASA (18). This request was made on the same day he requested James Webb (19) to begin Kennedy's peace overture to the Russians via joint space exploration. Webb, a board member of the intelligence community, likely interpreted Kennedy's program to mean the sharing of classified UFO data under which the current directive was forbidden. In Kennedy's top secret memorandum (20), he outlined for Angleton specific items he wished to have disclosed to Webb, such as "[to] have the high threat cases reviewed with the purpose of identification of bona fide as opposed to the classified CIA and USAF sources (21)." Also, "that we make a clear distinction between the known and unknowns in the event the Soviets try to mistake our extended cooperation as a cover for intelligence gathering of their defense and space programs (22)."

Finally, Kennedy wanted Angleton to, "arrange a program of data sharing with NASA mission directors in their defensive responsibilities (23)." This was unprecedented and totally unacceptable to Angleton and the CIA. Here Kennedy was requesting the Central Intelligence Agency, the agency that he swore he would "break into a thousand pieces" to just hand over the most guarded secret ever. This memo was passed on to William Colby (24) who indicated to someone in Angleton's staff using a hand written note that said, "Response from Colby, Angleton has MJ directive" and is dated November 20, 1963, just two days before Kennedy died. It seems that Kennedy's request bounced around from Angleton's desk possibly seeking consensus on the request or passing the buck back to Angleton. In either case, it was a hot potato for which Angleton had to deal with. It is also significant that Kennedy's NSAM No. 271 was the last coming from Kennedy's desk just before he left Washington for Dallas.

What the real significance of this remains buried somewhere within the CIA, and Angleton spent many a day trying to figure out who ordered Kennedy's execution. Was Angleton set up, or did he unintentionally supply the needed ingredient for the murder of the century (25)? In either case, the secret(s) remained safe largely in part because of his relationships with Allen Dulles and Richard Helms (next chapters) who allowed him "knock-on-the-door" access thereby circumventing the structured CIA hierarchy.

The legend of James Jesus Angleton--and his "wilderness of mirrors" as he often referred to as his daunting task of protecting vital state secrets--faded into obscurity on 11 May 1987. Perhaps Jim was not the real bad guy in the counterintelligence game. Perhaps, he was its victim (26), (27).

References/Footnotes

(1) September 25, 1943 OSS memo released through the FOIA in September 1989.

(2) U.S. Senate Select Committee to Study Government Operations with Respect to Intelligence Activities, Final report, Book VI, April 23, 1976, pp. 154-55.

(3) JJA personal records. Angleton took a seven-month leave of absence to remain in Tucson, AZ, for unspecified reasons not substantiated by the need to be with his wife and family as is believed by other writers; see Angleton's absence from CIA Washington headquarters during May through December 1947; *COLD WARRIOR JAMES JESUS ANGLETON: THE CIA'S MASTER SPY CATCHER* by Tom Mangold, Touchstone Book published by Simon & Schuster, 1991, p. 361.

(4) The National Security Council on December 12, 1947, had adopted measures to counter the espionage and counterespionage threat as specified in NSCID 1 and later amended in NSCID 5 that authorized the Director of Central Intelligence to "conduct all organized Federal espionage and counterespionage operations." According to CIA historian Arthur B. Darling, atomic weapons research became an overriding issue and coordination within the Office of Scientific Research and Development. With the AEC, through CIA consultant Dr. H.P. Robertson and using General Vandenberg's directive containing an agreement between Dr. Vannevar Bush and others, facilitated the transfer of Manhattan Engineering District files to the Director of Central Intelligence for proper collection of foreign atomic energy research. Secret OSO activities in this area was not allowed to fall into administrative control of the AEC nor the FBI which Vandenberg thought should always remain within CIA intelligence operations: *THE CENTRAL INTELLIGENCE AGENCY: AN INSTRUMENT OF GOVERNMENT To 1950* by Arthur B. Darling, Penn State Press, 1990, pp.197-239.

(5) The term "U.F.O." as defined by Air Force intelligence directives is used to reflect unconventional aircraft and missiles and not interplanetary spacecraft.

(6) CIA FOIA response letter dated March 26, 1976 to July 14, 1975: FOIA request made by Ground Saucer Watch of Phoenix, AZ, in which it stated that the NSC tasked the CIA a requirement to determine the actual UFO threat. The CIA responded through the Office of Scientific Intelligence by creating the Intelligence Advisory Committee to study the threat aspects. Military members of the IAC fought vigorously to maintain participation in areas relating to AEC intelligence collection and the Joint Chiefs of Staff

represented by General Todd (who is mentioned in a FBI memo regarding JSC ignorance of flying saucer data in 1947) was at odds with the CIA about the duplication of efforts by the military intelligence division in producing UFO intelligence data for the IAC: *THE CENTRAL INTELLIGENCE AGENCY: AN INSTRUMENT OF GOVERNMENT To 1950* by Arthur B. Darling. Penn State Press, 1990, pp. 349-356.

(7) The KGB, the Committee for State Security; a non-military arm of the Soviet Intelligence Service. The GRU was the military arm. The KGB received its title in 1954. When mentioning the Russian Intelligence Service, LGB and GRU are referenced genetically to include both organizations.

(8) This remarkable fact is substantiated in the mistaken downgraded Top Secret Canadian Department of Transport Intra-Department Correspondence from Wilbert B. Smith to Dr. Robert I. Sarbacher, an American physicist and Science Consultant in the Guidance & Control Panel. Dated 21 November, 1950. Smith acknowledge that UFO studies were "considered by the United States authorities to be of tremendous significance," and that the "matter is the most classified subject in the United States Government, rating higher that the H-bomb.

(9) September 24, 1947 Top Secret/MAJIC EYES ONLY "Project WHITE HOT" Preliminary Estimate in Five Parts (Unacknowledged by the U.S. Government): *THE MAJESTIC DOCUMENTS* by Dr. Robert M. Wood, Ph.D. and Ryan S. Wood, Wood & Wood Enterprises, 1998, pp. 43-81.

(10) 25 November, 1955 Top Secret memorandum from Rear Admiral Edwin T. Layton, Deputy Director for Intelligence, The Joint Staff, to the Chairman, Joint Chiefs of Staff, ref. J.C.S. 1712/5. This report deals with the Burgess-MacLean defection after it was learned that sensitive weapons research information had been sent to Moscow through diplomatic means and the CIA was informed of the defection in which Angleton was devastated to learn that Kim Philby, a long standing friend of British intelligence, was part of the spy ring.

(11) Unacknowledged June 28, 1961 Top Secret National Security Memorandum from President John F. Kennedy to Allen Dulles, Director of Central Intelligence; Subject: Review of MJ-12 Intelligence Operations as they relate to Cold War Psychological Warfare Plans. It is a one line request that says, "I would like a brief summary from you at your earliest convenience."

(12) Unacknowledged CIA Top Secret/MJ 12 Counterintelligence carbon copy draft directive from Director of Central Intelligence to MJ 1-7 with eight tabs on government watermark onion skin paper (circa 1961).

(13) Yuriy Ivanovich Norsenko was a Soviet KGB officer who defected in 1962 and Angleton had him detained, then emotionally tortured for three years believing the warning given by another KGB defector Anatoliy Mikaylovich Golitsyn. Golitsyn said that Norsenko was ordered to defect and act as a disinformation plant to spread misleading information to the CIA regarding Soviet capabilities and intentions. Later CIA analysis suggested that it was Golitsyn who was the real mole planted within the CIA, not Norsenko. Angleton was convinced that Golitsyn was a bona fide defector and Golitsyn's information was then used by Angleton and the subsequent CI mole hunt virtually destroyed the CIA's covert operations for some time.

(14) Top Secret CIA wiretap report dated 3 August, 1962 between Howard Rothberg and Marilyn Monroe with references to Project 40, MOON DUST, 5412, and MJ-12. The report was given to James Angleton and has his signature at the bottom right hand portion of the document establishing that CI was aware of Monroe's desire to blackmail the Kennedys with their indiscretions made to her while they were engaged in a sexual affair with her prior to August, 1962.

(15) FBI File Number 105-40018-1, formerly classified "Secret." CIA is copied on 19 August, 1955, FBI document from Mr. Dennis A. Flinn, Director, Office of Security, Department of State and copy sent to Director, Central Intelligence Agency with attention: Deputy Director, Plans, SECRET; declassified on 11 November 1978. Subject matter was redacted.

(16) *Crypt 33: The Saga of Marilyn Monroe-The Final Word*, by Adela Gregory and Milo Speriglio, Birch Lane Press, 1993.

(17) This would be amazing since no one in government knew that James Angleton worked for the CIA much less his existence since there were few pictures of Angleton and very few within the agency knew who he was and what he did. It is also interesting, that until his appearance before the Church Committee in 1975, the public did not know about Angleton nor his counterintelligence position at the CIA. His identity was kept secret for 20 years.

(18) National Security Action Memorandum No. 271 dated November 12, 1963 to the Administrator, National Aeronautics and Space Administration. Subject: Cooperation with the USSR on Outer Space Matters. President Kennedy instructs James Webb as Administrator of NASA to "assume personally the initiative and central responsibility within the Government for the development of a program of substantive cooperation with the Soviet Union in the field of outer space, including the development of specific technical proposals. I assume that you will work closely with the Department of State and other agencies as appropriate." Kennedy had requested an interim report on NASA's progress in this adventure by December 15, 1963. Of course, after he was killed, this program was never acted upon.

(19) It should be pointed out here that James E. Webb had served on President Truman's Psychological Warfare Strategy Board and had assisted in revising NSC 10/2 for the Office of Policy Coordination (Covert Operations) in 1948 for the CIA, and the Joint Chiefs of Staff for emergency plans in case of war. He also was the author of the "Webb Staff Study" that worked out cooperation between the military and the CIA concerning IAC intelligence sharing of foreign atomic research with the AEC which allowed the DCI prerogatives in the dissemination to key executive officials.. At one time, he had been considered for the DCI slot after Rear Admiral Hillenkoetter left office in 1950.

(20) "Top Secret" Kennedy memorandum to the Director [of Counter Intelligence], Subject: Classification review of all UFO intelligence files affecting National Security dated 12 November, 1963.

(21) Ibid.

(22) Ibid.

(23) Ibid.

(24) Ibid.

(25) "The Men Who Killed Kennedy" at: http://www.ufoconspiracy.com/ reports/kennedy_assassins_.htm.

(26) James Angleton Jr., Miami, FL, has been providing us with much needed support over the last few years. Many of the conversations have centered on his grandfather's personal notes which number in the thousands of pages according to Jim.

(27) Darren Edmunson (retired Air Force Major) comments on Angleton and an exchange program, see page 178 for Darren.

Subject: Re: James Jesus Angleton
Date: Sun, 12 Mar 2000 10:59:39 EST
From: SATCOMKID@aol.com
To: rigoletto@sprintmail.com

-Robert,
"According to my contacts, Angleton was never a member of MJ12. He might have been privy to some information from MJ12 but never a member. Angleton, in 1970, wrote a counterintelligence assessment of the UFO phenomena.
In this document, Angleton mentioned the Roswell incident, an incident in the New Mexican Desert in 1964 and an exchange program between EBEs and us in 1965 and 1969. This document was entitled, "Assessment Number 7."
I know Rick Doty read this along with some other former gov employees; maybe Ernie Kellerstrass and Tom Mack. The document was classified Top Secret, codeword, with limited distribution. I saw the document while assigned to AF Intel in the late 70s. Too bad we couldn't get our hands on this document. I'm sure it is tucked away in some obscure vault with CIA headquarters."

-Darren

Chapter 2

(3)

ALLEN W. DULLES, JFK, MJ-12, AND ZR/RIFLE

When candidate John F. Kennedy won the 1960 presidential election on November 7, Allen W. Dulles, then Director of Central Intelligence had already briefed Kennedy on three occasions exposing him to the world of covert operations of the CIA. Dulles had cultivated an intellectual relationship with the young Kennedy. USAF General Charles P. Cabell, Deputy Director of Central Intelligence, had also briefed Kennedy earlier in the summer of 1960 on certain political targets deemed critical by President Eisenhower to national security. For the young Kennedy, it would be an eye opener to the big league game of conspiracy, assassination, and political expediency. All this was necessary to maintain the U.S. intelligence power structure and the cold war diversion required by the military-industrial complex in its ongoing MJ-12 scientific and technical "black world" project programs.

One of the programs on the briefing agenda was ZR/RIFLE, the CIA's "Murder, Inc." which was a political assassination unit created by Vice President Richard M. Nixon in 1960 also known as "Project 40." This state- sanctioned assassination unit was the outgrowth of the ever expanding conflict between the CIA and KGB over the battle for minds and hearts of neutral countries. The neutral countries were always seeking ways to appease both spy agencies, yet, stay beneficiaries of both capitalist West and communist East blocs seeking domination of the earth. In the background of the battling bull elephants in the tall grass, was the shared knowledge that a third contender existed for world domination, one without a face and identity. This third contender egged on the belligerents with the winner becoming subservient to this dark figure who controlled the world's economies and social structure for its own ends. So we had the "Secret Societies" of the world's powerful money institutions and the ruling elite of the Vatican's intelligentsia.

Dulles and the Power Structure

One of the slogans of the Central Intelligence Agency is found engraved in the main lobby of the Agency's headquarters building which reads, "The Truth Shall Make You Free" taken from the words of John 8:32 which establish the central theme of the intelligence elite for their craft. This "truth" is not found in the Holy Bible, but in the arrogant confidence held by the ruling elite. The "truth" is only possessed by those who have been initiated into the "secret" and who believed that all wisdom and power was granted by higher powers to those few who were the original members of the Cold War and the initiate of MJ-12 for determining future events. Allen Welsh Dulles was one of those who knew the "truth" and his connections to the world's intelligence elite made him a desirable ally to any president seeking policy decisions in the nuclear age.

James Jesus Angleton (Chapter 1, Section 2) fitted well into Allen Dulles' world view on intelligence for he had always enjoyed Dulles' full confidence. Without Angleton, Dulles would not have enjoyed the real time intelligence and gossip so crucial to CIA operations and the powerful elite. This was especially true since the liquid gossip was sourced from the chief of counterintelligence himself.

The connections between Allen Dulles and Joseph P. Kennedy and the secret elite societies are well known and documented. Joseph P. Kennedy, Ambassador to the Court of Saint James, presidential advisor, wealthy backer of Wall Street power brokers and associate of the America's royal families of the Rockefellers and Duponts, was a member of the elite. His influence on the young JFK was profound and instrumental in buying votes making sure his son was the Democratic Party's nominee for the 35th President of the United States.

Allen Dulles was an old acquaintance of Joseph Kennedy and had many contacts with the Kennedy patriarch as a Wall Street securities dealer.

UNITED STATES GOVERNMENT

Memorandum

TO : Mr. James J. Rowley
Chief, U.S. Secret Service

DATE: March 3, 1964

FROM : Mr. John McCone
Director, Central Intelligence Agency

CO-2-34,030

SUBJECT: Central Intelligence Report on the Assassination of John Kennedy

In response to the request made by your office on 24 February 1964 re: Lee Oswald's activities and assignments on behalf of this agency and Federal Bureau of Investigation, there follows a narrative summary of the internal subversive activities of the Oswald subject.

I recommend that unless the Commission makes a specific request for specific information contained herein, that this information not be volunteered. This agency has reason to assume that some junior Commission staff members may be potential sources of leaks to the news media or to other agencies; due to the highly sensitive nature of the enclosed material, it would certainly be in the national interest to withhold it at this time - unless there is, of course, a specific request made.

It is my understanding that Mr. Hoover has certain additive information within his agency, which has been transferred to his own personal files for safekeeping; he concurs that no material should be voluntarily given to the Commission which might affect the status of field operatives or their safety. He is particularly concerned about the De Bruey memorandum, which Central Intelligence has obtained and which, I understand, you have obtained. It is imperative that this information, at least for the time, remain under wraps.

Oswald subject was trained by this agency, under cover of the Office of Naval Intelligence, for Soviet assignments. During preliminary training, in 1957, subject was active in aerial reconnaissance of mainland China and maintained a security clearance up to the "confidential" level. His military records during this period are open to your agency and I have directed they be forwarded to the Commission.

Subject received additional indoctrination at our own Camp Peary site from September 8 to October 17, 1958, and participated in a few relatively minor assignments until arrangements were made for his entry into the Soviet Union in September 1959. While in the Soviet Union, he was on special assignment in the area of Minsk. It would not be advantageous at this time to divulge the specifics of that assignment; however, if you wish this information, it can

Figure 2: Leaked Oswald Memo

The elder Kennedy was even on the civilian commissions that studied and offered recommendations for the use of the CIA. Dulles was often invited to the Kennedy family compound and the Palm Beach mansion of Charles Wrightsman, a wealthy oil and aerospace executive and close friend of Joseph Kennedy. Dulles became a member of the influential Council of Foreign Affairs (CFR) in 1922 and maintained membership until his death in 1969. He wrote many articles for "Foreign Affairs." Most importantly, Allen Dulles contributed a great deal of intelligence for the OSS on Nazi Germany. His intelligence network was responsible for the collapse and surrender of key German elements within their armed services. With the recruitment of General Reinhard Gehlen's Russian intelligence network for the CIA, Dulles became the most informed intelligence officer of that period.

One also has to remember that Allen Dulles had spent over 40 years in the cult of intelligence and was one of the original architects of the Central Intelligence Agency and the National Security Act of 1947. He continued as an intelligence adviser to President Johnson and was a member of the Warren Commission after the official retirement age of 70. Though considered inept and sometimes out of touch, he still maintained a presence among the "Old Guard" and his insights on foreign intelligence matters were still being sought after he left the Agency. His ability to steer the official investigation into the JFK assassination away from the Agency and promoting the "lone nut" gunman theory demonstrated his power. He was thereby able to control the findings of the Warren Commission and pin the guilt on Lee Harvey Oswald. Oswald was, in all probability, acting as an undercover intelligence agent controlled by U.S. Attorney General Robert F. Kennedy working with a CIA-operated clandestine political action unit known as ZR/RIFLE (see declassified/leaked Oswald Memo, Figure 2, page 41). We think Oswald infiltrated its assassination team that was later turned against President Kennedy, but then Oswald was betrayed by CIA operatives and set up as "the patsy" for the assassination.

Allen Dulles, JFK, and the Outer Space Connection

Since its inception in 1947, the CIA was engaged in advancing the art of reconnaissance especially over the old Soviet Union. The CIA was also busy debunking the many "flying saucer" reports being reported to the USAF. Informed speculation had circulated among upper air intelligence officers that some foreign power must have owned them, but suspicions had been diverted away from the CIA. In 1953, Allen Dulles had been briefed on the situation and a year later appointed MIT professor Richard Bissel to personally oversee the CIA's overhead spy program which led to the establishment of the highly classified research center called "Watertown" (Dulles' birthplace) more popularly known as Area 51 north of Nellis AFB, NV (see, Section 3, Chapter 4). It had been rumored that shortly after Kennedy became president, Dulles arranged a tour of the secret test facility. There he was shown extraterrestrial hardware from the 1947 White Sands UFO that allegedly was recovered by the military as well as other artifacts. That incident has become the focus of considerable controversy as much as the famous Roswell incident.

In 1958, Allen Dulles was handed the responsibility by President Eisenhower to run the first U.S. spy reconnaissance satellite program called CORONA. This was a full three years before NASA put up a manned space flight mission. During the same period, Dulles arranged for the drafting of National Security Council Action Memorandum 1846 which was followed by a full blown national strategy for a space intelligence program under NSC 5814/1, "Preliminary U.S. Policy in Outer Space" giving the CIA exclusive access to the program management. NSC 5814/1 encompassed more than just overhead reconnaissance: It included technology integration of very advanced extraterrestrial communications and navigation systems plus classified lunar stations and maintenance-and-supply space shuttles envisioned in 1949 as part of "Operation ADAM and EVE" (next section), and the USAF component of the Department of Defense's overall anti-UFO defense project.

Truman's Adam & Eve Commission 1949

Figure 3

In 1949, President Truman created two secret commissions. These commissions were to meet privately without recording any of the commission's business. The commissions were code named "Adam and Eve." The first commission, Adam was to study the idea of releasing some information to the public. Adam was headed by a low level presidential aid Phillip Keaton (very much an unknown) with some education in science. The findings of the Adam commission consisted of the following statement:

"In this matter, public opinion must be recognized as a factor of considerable importance, even if clearly affirmative, might have the effect of placing before the American people a moral question of vital historical significance at a time when the full security impact of the question had not become apparent. If this decision is to be made by the American people, it should be made in the circumstances of an actual disclosure of the existence of space beings that had visited Earth. In other words, the American public might hesitate to believe in the existence of space beings unless the American Government showed proof." The source quoted this paragraph from a document that he was allowed to read. The document was classified codeword, dated 1 Dec 49.

The second commission "Eve" was chaired by no other than General Curtis E. LeMay. The second commission's goal was to plan a defense against an "alien attack." The summaries of Eve's findings were that: "Atomic bombs would be required to repel a space alien attack." What's interesting in this statement was the decision by President Truman to proceed at a record pace on the production of atomic weapons that could be released in space. General LeMay predicted it would take the United States 10 years to develop such a delivery system. President Truman wanted it developed in 5 years. In fact, in 1959, the first Atlas ICBMs were targeted for deep space. SIOP Plan 355 was developed to counter any space based alien invasion (Note: Remember all those "B-grade" movies made in the '50s about hostile "aliens?"). David Lilienthal, the first Atomic Energy Commission Chairman, was in charge of the production of enough atomic weapons to counter any anticipated alien threat. Rear Admiral Daniel Gallery and Air Force Lieutenant General Harold Harmon were also involved in this project. A Clarence L. Johnson, design engineer, was tasked with developing a delivery system that could send a Mark 3 atomic weapon into space. In 1948-49, there were fewer than 50 atomic bombs in the arsenal and none of these were assembled. The Mark 3 plutonium bombs, like the one dropped at Nagasaki, required more than 39 men over two days to assemble. The bombs were so large and heavy, with each weighing 10,000 pounds, that the delivery system had to be capable of sending this heavy weapon into space. As a result of the "Eve's" commission findings, atomic weapons production was increased three-fold. Of course, this decision coincided with the Soviet build up.

In 1964, after the first "alien encounter" (Trinity Site, or it could have been Area 17 at White Sands), the decision to defend America against an alien invasion was down played. Although we still had SIOP Plan 355, it was not seriously considered after the alien encounter.

Richard Helms (ex CIA Director, deceased in October 2002) supplied much of this information according to Rick Doty.

Continuing from page 44: In 1960, the CIA had emerged as the most powerful intelligence agency, as Operation MJTWELVE ascended to the top of the list of intelligence priorities with the Soviet ICBM threat taking a close second. Allen Dulles, as a member of the MJ-12 and 5412 committees found it necessary to withhold vital information on the CIA and the NSA's communications intelligence (COMINT) involving psychological warfare and technical intelligence (TECHINT) operations against the Soviet military infrastructure. This was considered Special Access Required (SAR) and sensitive compartmented intelligence (SCI) classified "Top Secret Level 3" information. During the October 1962 Cuban missile crises, the Executive Committee (EXCOM) advised Kennedy that the Soviets might deploy similar decoy devices (flying saucers) in an effort to counter the U.S. Atlas missile forces based in Turkey (also see reference 5, Chapter 2 for EXCOM). President Kennedy, reeling from the scathing U.S. and foreign press barrage leveled at his administration's handling of the CIA-backed April 1961 (Operation MONGOOSE) Cuban refugee invasion, ordered Dulles to provide him a full review of all MJ-12 Intelligence Operations related to Psychological Warfare Plans (1). Such disclosure of the CIA's highest classified intelligence had put Allen Dulles at the center of blame for botching an embarrassing invasion. Kennedy had already set in motion mechanisms to strip the CIA of all paramilitary covert operations. Now Dulles was being forced to expose Kennedy to the "family jewels" of the CIA's most guarded secret. This might have compromised the whole U.S. intelligence community and MJ-12. The end result of that June 28, 1961 directive appears to be a full Operational Review prepared by Dulles dated 5 November 1961 (Figure 4). In this one page Figure 4 document, Dulles tells JFK that indeed some UFOs may be of "non-terrestrial origin" and that "I cannot divulge pertinent data on some of the more sensitive aspects of MJ-12 activities which have been deemed properly classified under the Atomic Energy Act of 1954." This page one of a full operational review is a retype of the original document and from research has all the indications of being authentic.

President Kennedy began to back away from nuclear confrontation with the Soviets, the Communist insurgent wars in Laos and Vietnam, the dismantling of the CIA and the firing of Allen Dulles, Richard Bissell, and General Cabell. Instead, he began to assume control and reorganize the space program. On 26 May 1962, President Kennedy requested a classified directive be written up by the Secretary of State to the Department of Defense, CIA, NASA, AEC and science advisers which said:

The President is concerned about possible attacks on the U.S. Space Program at the forthcoming session of the U.N. Outer Space Committee and the General Assembly. Please develop positions on the following questions in consultation with DOD, CIA, NASA, AEC, and the science advisor:

1. How do we deal with charges the United States is seeking a military domination in space and plans to use space to launch weapons of mass destruction?

2. [Sanitized]

3. How do we defend the past and prospective space experiments (high-altitude nuclear test Project West Ford), which may have lasting effects in space and impair the free use of space by other nations?

4. How do we dispel foreign misapprehensions arising from our bitter domestic debate...and charges that the legislation is somehow inconsistent

TOP SECRET

SENSITIVE

5 November 1961

Operations Review
by Allen W. Dulles

THE MJ-12 PROJECT

The Overview. In pursuant to the Presidential National Security Memorandum of June 28, 1961, the U.S. intelligence operations against the Soviet Union are currently active in two broad areas; aircraft launch vehicles incorporating ELINT and SIGINT capabilities; and balloon borne decoys with ECM equipment.

The Situation. The overall effectiveness about the actual Soviet response and alert status is not documented to the point where U.S. intelligence can provide a true picture of how Soviet air defenses perceive unidentified flying objects.

Informational sources have provided some detail on coded transmissions and tactical plans whose reliability is uncertain, and thus, do not give us precise knowledge of Soviet Order of Battle. Current estimates place Soviet air and rocket defenses on a maximum alert footing with air operations centered on radar and visual verification much the same as ours.

Future psychological warfare plans are in the making for more sophisticated vehicles whose characteristics come very close to phenomena collected by Air Force and NSA elements authorized for operations in this area of intelligence.

Basis for Action. Earlier studies indicated that Americans perceived U.F.O. sightings as the work of Soviet propaganda designed to convince U.S. intelligence of their technical superiority and to spread distrust of the government. CIA conducted three reviews of the situation utilizing all available information and concluded that 80% of the sighting reports investigated by the Air Force's Project Blue Book were explainable and posed no immediate threat to national security. The remaining cases have been classified for security reasons and are under review. While the possibility remains that true U.F.O. cases are of non-terrestrial origin, U.S. intelligence is of the opinion that they do not constitute a physical threat to national defense. For reasons of security, I cannot divulge pertinent data on some of the more sensitive aspects of MJ-12 activities which have been deemed properly classified under the 1954 Atomic Energy Act of 1954.

I hope this clarifies the necessity to keep current operations with CIA activities in sensitive areas from becoming official disclosure. From time to time, updates will be provided through NIE as more information becomes available.

(Signed) Allen W. Dulles

This document contains information affecting
the national defense of the United States within
of the Espionage Laws, Title 18,
U. S. C., Section 793 and 794. The transmission
or the revelation of its contents in any manner
to an unauthorized person is prohibited by law.
Exempted from automatic regrading: DoD 5200.10

This document contains ____ pg
Copy No. of copies

Figure 4: Page one of a full operational review.

with U.N. statements. The president would like to see the positions developed to deal with these questions.

McGeorge Bundy

While the intelligence community was formulating plans on how to deal with the president's new direction on the CIA's space program and MJ-12 intelligence operations, Kennedy wrote a private letter to Nikita S. Khrushcev. In this letter he expressed relief that the nuclear confrontation arising over Khrushcev's placing of offensive missiles on Castro's Cuba had ended. Dated 14 December 1962, Kennedy revealed a new channel of communications which was later intercepted by the NSA:

Dear Mr. Chairman:

I was glad to have your message of December 11th and to know that you believe, as we do, that we have come to the final stage of the Cuban affair between us, the settlement of which will have significance for our future relations and for our ability to overcome other difficulties. I wish to thank you for your expression of appreciation of the understanding and flexibility we have tried to display.

With regard to your reference to the confidential channels set up between us, I can assure you that I value them. I have not concealed from you that it was a serious disappointment to me that dangerously misleading information should have come through these channels before the recent crisis...

The 12 November, 1963 JFK Memo and NSAM 271

According to an alleged "Top Secret" memorandum (refer back to Chapter 1) leaked to Tim Cooper (2), Kennedy had requested the Director of Central Intelligence, John McCone, and the Deputy Director of Counterintelligence, James J. Angleton, to review all classified CIA and USAF UFO projects (supposedly issued by Kennedy just 10 days before he was gunned down in the streets of Dallas, TX). They were to provide this data to James Webb, NASA's administrator, for a joint space exploration program with the Soviets. If true, this document may be the most significant document attesting to the reality of the super-secret MJ-12 intelligence organization created by President Harry S. Truman in 1947 and perhaps provide us with one of the prime reasons and/or motives for Kennedy's assassination in Dallas and the continuing cover-up.

In it, Kennedy wanted to convince Khrushchev of his sincerity by breaking down barriers and aligning the U.S. intelligence community with the Soviet space program. This would provide a basis for trust thus ending the mistrust between the U.S. and Soviet Union and perhaps ending the Cold War.

In a surprising discovery made by several researchers in 1999, a relevant JFK document was discovered that supports the contents of the 12 November, 1963 "Top Secret" UFO memo. Issued on the same day, President Kennedy signed National Security Action Memorandum No. 271 (NSAM 271) directing James Webb, administrator of the National Aeronautics and Space Administration, to "assume personally the initiative and central responsibility within the Government for the development of a program of substantive cooperation with the Soviet Union in the field of outer space." This would be a first in the Cold War standoff between the United States and the Soviet Union of any technical and scientific exchange. This was also an unbelievable, surreal threat to the U.S. intelligence community, or to MJ-12 and an untenable position for NASA. The shock waves that went through the cubicles of the CIA and the corridors of the Pentagon must have been unbearable to the military-industrial complex and MJ-12. Kennedy had already made many enemies when he instructed the Chairman of the Joint Chiefs of Staff to assume all paramilitary covert operations from the CIA through his NSAM numbers 55 and 56. This essentially would take the CIA out of the covert world of operations and removed Allen Dulles from his power base as Director of Central Intelligence. It is no coincidence that on 28 June 1961, the same day NSAM 55 was issued, he ordered Allen Dulles to disclose the covert operations of MJ-12 intelligence. For Dulles, it was the end of his career and his job as the President's intelligence officer.

In the wording of NSAM 271, Kennedy explicitly advised James Webb that NASA would include "the development of specific technical proposals" and "cooperation in lunar landing programs." Kennedy's goal was further expanded through a "means of continuing dialog between the scientists of both countries." This substantiates other documents leaked to Tim Cooper that secret negotiations had reached a level of confidence in dealing with the UFO threat that existed and briefly mentioned in other secret executive communications between Kennedy and Khrushchev.

ZR/Rifle, the Conspiracy to kill President Kennedy

Called "Murder, Inc." by President Lyndon B. Johnson, the CIA's political action program known by its cover name ZR/Rifle was ordered activated by President Kennedy to eliminate Fidel Castro and was managed by his brother U.S. Attorney General Robert F. Kennedy from the Justice Department. In October 1963, while Dulles was moving his personal items out of his office at CIA headquarters, he was ordered by Kennedy to put Operation MONGOOSE—the assassination of Castro and as many of his top aides as possible—into readiness. What President Kennedy and his brother did not know was that foreign hit men had been approached through intermediaries on behalf of U.S. intelligence to kill an American politician in the United States. Kennedy had requested MJ-12 UFO intelligence and a proposal by 1 February 1964 in anticipation of winning the presidential election in his own right. He would be announcing the pullout of U.S. military advisers from Laos and Vietnam by the end of the year and then perhaps disclosing the classified UFO program to the public. He would also engage NASA in a joint lunar exploration program with the Soviets thereby ending the nuclear arms race all in his second term. With Castro out of the way and liberating Cuba, Kennedy's popularity would guarantee his presidency for another four years thus paving the way for his brother, Robert Kennedy, the 1968 presidential election and a Democratic controlled White House for the 1970s. Whether JFK's later discovered extensive use of pain killers for back pain or his extra-marital affairs would have changed all that is a matter of continued historical debate and speculation.

But, on November 22, 1963, all those hopes for JFK and the world ended with three or more gun shots. No Vietnam pull out, no reorganization of the CIA, and no UFO disclosures. Allen Dulles was then free to finish his work on the Warren Commission and forever hence keep those secrets that were deemed "Exempt from Disclosure" as Richard Helms would do as we shall see in the next chapter.

References/Footnotes

(1) JFK National Security Directive, June 28, 1961. Review of MJ-12 Intelligence Operations as they relate Cold War Psychological Warfare Plans, http://209.132.68.98/pdf/kennedy_ciadirector.pdf

(2) JFK Memorandum for the Director, Central Intelligence Agency. November 12, 1963. Classification review of all UFO intelligence file affecting national security, http://209.132.68.98/pdf/kennedy_cia.pdf

(3) **Figure 1**: This is Allen Dulles's identification card from the Office of Strategic Services (OSS), the United States' intelligence gathering agency during World War II. Dulles was stationed in Bern, Switzerland for much of the war where he gained his reputation as a spymaster.

Second illustration is the back of Allen Dulles's identification card from the Office of Strateic Services, the United States intelligence gathering agency during World War II, signed by William Donovan. Donovan drafted the plans for the OSS and was its director during the war see, http://infoshare1.princeton.edu/libraries/firestone/rbsc/finding_aids/adulles/index.html.

4) Dulles biographical references.

a) *Allen Dulles: Master of Spies*, James Srodes, 2000, Regnery Publishing, Inc.

Chapter 3

RICHARD HELMS: DIRECTOR OF CENTRAL INTELLIGENCE

"Richard Helms was briefed into the subject of UFOs in the early days. He knew about Roswell and knew the involvement of the CIA from around 1950 to the 1970s. Helms knew the NSA involvement with programs to capture ET signals."

—Rick Doty

"The Central Intelligence Agency," Allen Dulles once told Congress "should be directed by a relatively small, but elite corps of men with a passion for anonymity and a willingness to stick at that particular job (1) ." Richard Helms, the eighth Director of Central Intelligence (1966-1973) had those qualities. He died in Washington on October 23rd 2002 at the age of 89. He was among the last of a dwindling group of trailblazers like James Jesus Angleton and Allen Dulles (Chapters 1 & 2) who dominated American intelligence for much of the Cold War, but who like his cohorts was deeply steeped in covert UFO operations. When Helms started his career with the new agency 55 years ago, he was one of a group of young veterans of clandestine warfare during World War II. They chose to stay in the secret world to fight a new and, in many ways, a more formidable enemy. Seemingly, Helms was a natural at managing secret operations. He rose from desk officer to DCI and came to represent a new type of government professional: The career intelligence officer steeped in the culture of clandestine activities—like Majestic-12 —and devoted to the agency as an institution. Intelligence work, Helms would later say, was "not merely . . . a job, but rather . . . a calling."

Richard Helms was born in 1913 into a family of means and international connections. He grew up in the middle class suburbs of Philadelphia and New York. One of his brothers described their youth as "conventional upper-middle class, well educated, well traveled, interested in good schools and sports, and with a social life centering on the country club (1)." Helms took part of his schooling at academies in Switzerland and Germany and became fluent in French and German. In 1931, he entered Williams College and majored in literature and history. He became class president and head of the school paper, and was voted "most respected," "best politician," and "most likely to succeed."

Wartime with the OSS

In 1942, Helms joined the US Naval Reserve, received a commission as a lieutenant, and worked in the Eastern Sea Frontier headquarters in New York City, plotting the locations of German submarines in the Atlantic Ocean. A former wire service colleague approached him about working for the new Office of Strategic Services in its Morale Operations Branch, which produced "black" propaganda. In 1943, the Navy transferred Helms to the OSS in Washington.

Helms was able to organize infiltrations of agents behind German lines to spy and set up resistance networks. Late in the war, he was "forward deployed" to Paris. Then, after V-E Day, he moved on to Luxembourg and Germany where he was made deputy chief of the espionage element in Wiesbaden. In August 1945, he was transferred to a similar job in Berlin under Allen Dulles. From there, he tracked down Nazi sympathizers and war criminals, collected information on stolen goods, traced German scientists, and monitored Soviet military misdeeds.

A Life's Work

After President Truman abolished the OSS in late 1945, Helms moved into the Berlin office of the Strategic Services Unit, a carryover operational organization warehoused in the War Department. In December, he came back to Washington (for good, as it turned out) to run the central Europe branch of the short-lived Central Intelligence Group. Then in late 1947, he took a somewhat similar position in the new CIA's Office of Special Operations which was the same office that James Angleton worked in; as a senior aide, he undoubtedly kept Helms informed of the most guarded secrets and most likely UFOs were on the list. This is reinforced by a conversation on March 26, 2000 between Tim Cooper and James Angleton Jr. where JA, Jr. said that his grandfather James Jesus Angleton (JJA) helped establish MJ MAJESTIC-12 CI operations before he was appointed Director of Counter-Intelligence (2).

Since its inception in 1947, the CIA was engaged in advancing the art of reconnaissance especially over the old Soviet Union and UFOs (reference Chapters 1 and 2). In the same breath, the CIA was busy debunking the many "flying saucer" reports being reported to the USAF. Informed speculation had circulated among upper air intelligence officers that some foreign power must have operated them, but suspicions were always diverted away from the CIA. However, according to a 1975 FOIA release, Walter B. Smith (3) who was the DCI before Dulles, had such an intense interest in the UFO subject, he went so far as asking for cooperation between all the military services, the Research and Development Board of the DOD, the Psychological Strategy Board and other government agencies as appropriate (4). We can only surmise from chapters 1 and 2 that this interest never waned even up to today, and it's not too difficult to say that roughly 90 percent of all things done by the CIA are done covertly.

The covertness of the CIA was keenly brought to the surface by the then new CIA Director Porter J. Goss who in 2003, before the 9-11 Commission, said that the classification policy was "dysfunctional." "There's a lot of gratuitous classification going on," he said at a May 23, 2003 hearing of the Commission. "We over-classify very badly."

In 1962, John McCone, DCI, who had replaced Allen Dulles the year before, selected Helms as the DDP, Deputy Directorate of Plans, which proved to be important symbolically and substantively. It quieted many of the rumblings from the clandestine service careerists after the Bissell and Dulles ousters, and allayed their fears that McCone, a shipping and construction

tycoon, was bent on running the agency like a big business. Helms'
promotion also signaled a shift in emphasis from covert action to espionage—
a reorientation with which he wholeheartedly agreed.

After McCone resigned in 1965 and was replaced by Adm. William
Raborn, President Lyndon Johnson appointed Helms Deputy Director of
Central Intelligence (DDCI) to give him more Washington seasoning before
elevating him to the top job. When that occurred a year later, LBJ handled it in
his inimitable way by announcing it at a press conference without asking
Helms first; the DCI-designate heard about the *fait accompli* from an
administration official only a short time before President Johnson told the
media.

Helm's Style

Urbane, cool, shrewd, sure-footed, tight-lipped (kept all the little dirty secrets)
controlled, discreet—such adjectives appear frequently in colleagues and
friends' recollections of Helms. On the job, he was serious and demanding.
An efficient worker and delegator, he left his desk clear at the end of the day
(almost always before 7 p.m.), feeling assured that the trustworthy
subordinates he had carefully chosen could pick up the details and handle any
problems. According to a colleague, "Helms was a fellow who by and large
gave the people who worked with him his confidence . . . his instinct was to
trust them. . . ."

Sometimes, however, Helms' hands-off style and deference to deputies
worked against him. In the area of covert action, for example, more
"proactive" management on his part might have averted the near-collapse of
the CIA's political action capabilities after the agency's network of
international organizations, propaganda outlets, proprieties, foundations, and
trusts were exposed in a 1967 *Ramparts'* magazine article. Similarly, in the
area of counter-intelligence, Helms accorded (as mentioned before) the chief
of the CI Staff DD/CI James Angleton, much leeway in vetting assets,
dealing with defectors and suspected double agents, and searching for
"moles" inside the Agency—despite the costs of disrupting legitimate
operations and tarnishing officers' careers (5).

Helms declined a presidential request to submit his resignation after the 1972 elections, not wanting to set a precedent that he thought would politicize the position of DCI. After he was forced out in 1973— he believed that Nixon was very angry at him for refusing to use the CIA in the Watergate cover up—Helms spent several years coping with controversies ensuing in part from some of his acts of omission and commission while at the agency. He became a lightning rod for criticism of the CIA during its "time of troubles" in the mid-1970s. He was called back many times from his ambassadorial post in Tehran to testify before investigative bodies about assassination plots, domestic operations, drug testing, the destruction of records, and other activities of dubious legality and ethicality known collectively as the "Family Jewels." He responded to inquiries about them cautiously, sometimes testily, as he tried to walk the increasingly fuzzy line between discretion and disclosure.

Helms ran into legal troubles resulting from his judgment about when and when not to reveal secrets. Testifying before the Senate Foreign Relations Committee just after leaving the agency, he firmly denied that the CIA had tried to influence the outcome of the Chilean presidential election in 1970. Helms described his quandary this way: "If I was to live up to my oath and fulfill my statutory responsibility to protect intelligence sources and methods from unauthorized disclosure, I could not reveal covert operations to people unauthorized to learn about them." He eventually pleaded no contest to charges of not testifying "fully, completely and accurately" to the committee.

To the end, Richard Helms was "at the table." He remained privately engaged in public affairs for so many years after leaving Langley that it is easy to forget how long ago he entered the secret world and how far he traveled within it as Rick Doty will testify to in the next chapter. His now published memoir, "*A Look Over My Shoulder, A Life in the CIA*," will enable us to accompany him on that journey, but there were never any public statements by him on the subject of UFOs as everything was done covertly except for personal "leaks" to friends (6). Perhaps we can better understand the man publicly, but not privately, who declared at the depths of the agency's travail in the mid-1970s, "I was and remain proud of my work there. I believed in the importance to the nation of the function that the Agency served. I still do without regrets, without qualms, without apology." If he could speak to us now, he would say the same—and probably add, "Let's get on with it," and so we shall with Rick Doty in Chapter 4.

References/Footnotes

(1) Remember that Allen Dulles had spent over 40 years in the cult of intelligence and was one of the original architects of the Central Intelligence Agency and the National Security Act of 1947.

(2) Tim Cooper writes that on the 26th of March 2000 James Angleton, Jr. said that the piece this author wrote on his grandfather was "accurate and interesting (Chapter 1)." We had a 45-minute chat on the telephone in which he stated that Mangold (Cold Warrior) did terrible coverage on the CIA's CI staff and irritated his family for years. He is holding his grandad's papers which his father gave him for safekeeping, and some Dulles files which Angleton took from CIA headquarters. According to JA, Jr., Angleton helped establish MJ MAJESTIC-12 CI operations BEFORE he was appointed DD of CI. He said that NSA runs the show pretty much now, but the CIA and DIA still have COMINT channels and sources. He wants to see my carbon copy of the (1960s) CIA/MJ-12 directive as I'm using it as a bargaining chip to see some of his holdings.

(3) In 1950, President Harry Truman appointed Army Lieutenant General Walter Bedell Smith, a tough and respected military officer-diplomat with impressive credentials as the new Director of Central Intelligence (DCI). During Bedell Smith's years, Angleton (Chapter 1) continued as chief of Staff "A" (foreign intelligence operations), one of four advisory staffs inside the CIA's clandestine arm.

(4) Walter B. Smith declassified CIA 1952 draft memos (next pages) which mention UFOs.

(5) Next to Allen Dulles, Angleton's most important and longest serving patron was Richard Helms, the legendary and consummate intelligence professional who served as DDO in 1962-'65 and DCI in 1966-'73. By the time he met Angleton, Helms had been a journalist and a clandestine intelligence officer in the OSS and in the interim postwar American intelligence organizations. After joining the CIA, he rose quickly, ending up near the top of the agency's clandestine directorate by the early 1950s.

 ER - 3 - 2808

MEMORANDUM TO: The Executive Secretary
                National Security Council

SUBJECT: Unidentified Flying Objects (Flying Saucers)

1. The Central Intelligence Agency has reviewed the current situation concerning unidentified flying objects which have caused extensive speculation in the press and have been the subject of concern to Government organizations. The Air Force, within the limitations of manpower which could be devoted to the subject, has thus far carried the full responsibility for investigating and analyzing individual reports of sightings. Since 1947, approximately 2000 official reports of sightings have been received and, of these, about 20% are as yet unexplained.

2. It is my view that this situation has possible implications for our national security which transcend the interests of a single service. A broader, coordinated effort should be initiated to develop a firm scientific understanding of the several phenomena which apparently are involved in these reports, and to assure ourselves that the incidents will not hamper our present efforts in the Cold War or confuse our early warning system in case of an attack.

3. I therefore recommend that this Agency and the agencies of the Department of Defence be directed to formulate and carry out a program of intelligence and research activities required to solve the problem of instant positive identification of unidentified flying objects. A draft of an appropriate directive is attached.

                                Walter B. Smith
                                Director

Inclosure

FILE COPY

JUN 2 1 1992

Declassified by _____ 0059
date 2 4 JAN 1975

Figure 2a: WBS memo page 1

D R A F T

NATIONAL SECURITY COUNCIL DIRECTIVE

SUBJECT: Unidentified flying objects

Pursuant to the provisions of Section 102 of the National Security Act of 1947 and for the purposes annunciated in Paragraphs d and e thereof, the National Security Council hereby authorizes and directs that:

1. The Director of Central Intelligence shall formulate and carry out a program of intelligence and research activities as required to solve the problem of instant positive identification of unidentified flying objects.

2. Upon call of the Director of Central Intelligence, Government departments and agencies shall provide assistance in this program of intelligence and research to the extent of their capacity provided, however, that the DCI shall avoid duplication of activities presently directed toward the solution of this problem.

3. This effort shall be coordinated with the military services and the Research and Development Board of the Department of Defense, with the Psychological Strategy Board and other Governmental agencies as appropriate.

4. The Director of Central Intelligence shall disseminate information concerning the program of intelligence and research activities in this field to the various departments and agencies which have authorized interest therein.

FILE COPY

JUN 2 1 1992

Declassified by ___ 0000
date 2 4 JAN 1975

Figure 2b: WBS Memo page 2

Angleton's longstanding friendships with Dulles and Helms were to become the most important factors in giving him freedom of movement within the CIA. He was extended such trust by his superiors that there was often a significant failure of executive control over his activities. The result was that his subsequent actions were performed without bureaucratic interference. The simple fact was that if Angleton wanted something done, it was done. He had the experience, the patronage, and the clout.

In the '60s the Counterintelligence Staff, for example, had its very own secret slush fund, which Angleton tightly controlled. This fund gave him easy access to a large amount of money that was never audited (as other such funds were). Angleton argued that he would have to be trusted without outside accountability because it had been difficult to allow mere clerks to go through his accounts if only because sources would have to be revealed. The DCIs (including Helms) agreed to this unusual arrangement, which gave Angleton unique authority to run his own little operation without undue supervision. From *Cold Warrior* by Tom Mangold, 1991 page 52,

(6) This information reportedly came from Mr. R (Richard Helms) in March of 1999, EBEs 1, 2, and 3. This is in source's own words.

"While Ebe #1 was alive, there was apparently a failure to communicate between Ebe #1 and our military. They failed to ask Ebe #1 about the CR device or any other items aboard Ebe's spacecraft except one. Ebe explained their communication device. It was a small (12" x 9" x 2") device. It contained several small holes, two 4" antennas and two black inlayed "chips". Of course we didn't know the black items were a form of computer chips back then but we know that today. The communication device also had a series of lights that would alternate from left to right when an incoming signal was received. The lights would alternate from right to left when an out going signal was sent. What was interesting was how this device was powered. It was later learned that the communication device was connected to the CR [Crystal Rectangle, see Section 3 Chapter 3 for CR] by a small glass tube (fiber optics?). There were no wires within this glass tube [more like a crystal type material]. To the best of Mr. R's (Richard Helms) knowledge, they still haven't figured out how the power goes from the CR to the communication's device. Although we could not operate the communication's device, we used it to manufacture a device that was later used to communicate with the Ebens. Mr. R states the device was classified until the late '70s.; now the military uses it.

"Ebe #2 came in 1964, not 1974. He was here from 1964 until 1984. Ebe #3 came in 1979 and stayed until 1989." (Comment: or was it 1993?)

"This information has never been disclosed before. It should be held in the strictest of confidence (Code word and above). Ebe #1 had psychic powers! He was able to move items by just looking at them. He even moved one of our aircraft (an F-89 fighter) from a runway to a hanger!! [sic] He also had healing powers. He was able to move his right hand over an injury and cause the injury to heal [Similar to the scene in ET where ET moved pointed his finger at the cut in the boy's hand!] While at Los Alamos, Ebe #1 observed a construction project going on. A large crane was used to hoist steel beams from the ground to the top of a building under construction. Without anyone's clue, Ebe #1 moved his right hand over a steel beam and levitated it to the top of the building! Obviously, that impressed a lot of people. As you are probably aware, Ebe #1 could communicate by telepathy. But he could actually do more than that. He could read the thoughts of people before they were reading [sic] to express them! He had the ability to delve into the mind and bring out thoughts and dreams. Ironically, Ebe #2 and Ebe #3 did not have this ability. Ebe #2 had some psychic ability but not anywhere near Ebe #1's ability."

Chapter 4

RICHARD DOTY: AIR FORCE OFFICE OF SPECIAL INVESTIGATIONS (AFOSI) COUNTER-INTELLIGENCE and Raven Addendum, the Wilderness of Mirrors

Christopher Green MD, PhD in Neurophysiology now at Wayne State Medical Center in Michigan relates that many years ago one of his friends, Richard Helms, ex-CIA Director at the time, told him, "Always believe what Richard Doty tells you about UFOs."

I was born on February 15, 1950 in New York State and retired from the United States Air Force in November 1988 as a Master Sergeant. What you are about to read is some of my 20 years experience in the area of UFOs and aliens which today is just as much a surprise to me as it was back in July 1969 with my first encounter. Hype and exaggerations have been avoided at all costs so the following story might seem monotonous, but it is unpretentious. I certainly don't know all the facts and I assume that by this time some or a lot of the information you are about to read has changed.

So, where do I begin? Well, in August of 1968, I began my basic training at Lackland A.F.B., TX, which, lasted until November. After that I stayed at Lackland for a special duty assignment. After basic training, I went through air force security police school at Lackland. I then was assigned to the 1041st Combat Security Police Wing, where I went through 14 weeks of combat training in Hawaii. After training, I volunteered for a special duty assignment at Indian Springs AFB Nevada which required that I have a "Top Secret" clearance. There were a total of 10 security policeman selected for this TDY. After receiving our clearances ,we were flown to Indian Springs AFB.

Indian Springs AFB is located approximately 60 miles northwest of Las Vegas and contained tactical firing ranges used by combat aircraft. Approximately 15 miles southeast of Indian Springs was located a top secret Air Force facility and this is where my career as a security policeman began.

Upon my arrival at this special facility the 10 security policemen and I were given a Top Secret briefing by a USAF Colonel. The briefing was quite generic; no details of the special facility were given. All we were told was that the facility tested special aircraft. We were housed in a new air-conditioned building containing a theater, dining facility and a recreational area. My special duty was to guard a very large hangar estimated to be 3500 ft by 4000 ft and at least 100 ft in height. The hangar was located inside a high security fenced in area with two entry points. It was one of the largest hangars I'd ever seen. I was assigned to security flight "C." My supervisor was a Master Sergeant. We also had two air force officers, one captain and one lieutenant. Another flight of security policemen guarded the interior of the building. These security policemen were E-6 or higher. During an extremely hot July day in 1969 at ~9:00 a.m., and under very tight security, the hangar doors were opened. I was amazed at the size of the object located inside (this scene was depicted in Steven Spielberg's "Taken" which was televised on the Sci-Fi channel in December 2002). My first impression was that the object was a "flying saucer." It was pulled out of the hangar by a large USAF tug vehicle and because of my close proximity to the hangar door (about 50 ft), the object literally passed over my head. I was again stunned by its size as it was pulled out onto a runway. It sat on the runway for about an hour while several attempts were made to start it up, but it would not start. Technicians in white coveralls and civilian suits worked on the object for another hour. Finally, the large craft was pulled back into the hangar.

Later that afternoon, while off duty, I asked my supervisor what the object was. I was told it was an experimental aircraft. I joking replied that the object looked like a flying saucer. About that time, a man in civilian clothing asked me to meet with him in an unoccupied room.

Once inside, the room the civilian identified himself as Mr. Blake. Blake asked me what I knew about flying saucers. I mentioned that I had read some magazines, but that I was joking when I said the object looked like a flying saucer. Blake told me that he knew my uncle and how my uncle (Ed Doty) worked as an investigator on UFO sightings. I stated that I knew this and that my uncle had mentioned this to me in the past. Blake then said, "What if I told you that the object you saw today was a real flying saucer from another planet then what would you say?" I said I wouldn't know what to say. Blake laughed and then he told me not to mention this to anyone. Blake then escorted me to the door saying, "Airmen Doty, someday you'll know the true story about that object sitting in the big hangar." I simply nodded and left the room. Little did I know how right he would be?

I saw the large "flying saucer" again several more times in the next 45 days. However, it never did fly. The day prior to my departure the same Colonel who gave the initial briefing debriefed me. I flew back to Nellis then eventually back to Sheppard AFB. About two months before departing for Vietnam, my uncle (who had just been promoted) came to the base to visit me. I was instructed to get into civilian clothes and then he took me to the Officer's club for dinner. During the meal my uncle asked me about my temporary assignment to Indian Springs. I told him I saw something I wasn't sure about. He told me that indeed the object was a captured flying saucer and I was very surprised at the nonchalant way my uncle brought up the subject. I wondered whether it was safe to bring up this type of subject in the club, but my uncle told me not to worry.

For the next hour my uncle talked about the flying saucer in the hangar and about what the government really knew. Among the things that he told me was that the USAF had an alien in captivity, but the alien died several years ago. My uncle never spoke in specifics just general terms.

Comment: On 21 February 2003, Ed Doty stated to Robert Collins, "Robert: That conversation with my nephew occurred over 33 years ago. I don't remember much of the conversation. Richard had been assigned to a special security detail at the Nellis Test Site (NTS). He guarded a classified project. He arrived back at Sheppard, his host base. I was TDY at Sheppard and looked him up. I managed to get him into the O-Club for lunch. He told me about his ordeal at the Nevada Test Site (NTS). To the best of my knowledge, he did not discuss anything classified. That's all I remember. Ask Richard maybe he remembers the conversation, Best, Ed."

After returning from Vietnam I was stationed at McChord AFB in Washington State. In the fall of 1971, I was involved in a UFO incident that was described as "a thing" by two enlisted Air Force navigational site technicians. The "thing" was dressed in metallic coveralls and wearing a space helmet. After an investigation, of which nothing ever came of the whole incident, the subject was dropped.

In September 1976, after more overseas duty, I was stationed at Ellsworth AFB, SD, and assigned to the 44th Security Police Squadron. In this case the UFO incident as described in the DD 1569, Air Force Incident/Complaint Report, turned out to be a hoax and the sergeant involved in faking the DD 1569 was punished and dismissed from the Air Force.

In the spring of 1978, I was recruited by the Air Force Office of Special Investigations (AFOSI) to become an agent. I passed all the necessary requirements and tests and was sent to the AFOSI Academy in Washington, D.C. After successfully graduating from the academy, I was sent to District 17 OSI, Kirtland AFB New Mexico in May 1979.

Upon my arrival, I was given the standard briefing regarding the base and the surrounding area. I was assigned to the Base Investigative Detachment (BID). The BID was responsible for conducting investigations on base and the surrounding area. The mission of the OSI was to investigate all major crimes occurring on a military installation if the crime involved military personnel, equipment and/or property. During that first year, I was briefed into three (3) special programs. The first program involved the collection of intelligence and counter-intelligence information. The first part of the briefing was conducted at the Special Security Office (SSO) at the Air Force Weapon's Laboratory Kirtland AFB, Albuquerque, NM. The second part (second program) of the briefing pertained to the collection of information about UFOs. To my surprise and just prior to this second briefing, Mr. Blake entered the room. He reminded me of what he had said years earlier. I laughed and asked him if he could predict the future. I was also briefed into another very special (third) program that dealt with the safe guarding of the Air Force's high technology programs. Among the methods used to safeguard these programs was "disinformation."

During this briefing, I read from an official Air Force document about the history of the U.S. Government's involvement in the investigation of UFOs. I saw pictures of a crashed UFO that had been recovered in the desert of New

Mexico in the later 1940s (Roswell). I also read about a captured alien (EBE-1) that lived in New Mexico at Los Alamos National Labs from 1947 until his death in 1952. The historical account continued with information EBE-1 provided to the U.S. Government about space, our solar system, EBE-1's home planet, and about the future of the Universe. EBE-1 came from a planet, called "Sieu" in the star group of Zeta Reticuli. These are seen as fifth magnitude stars in the constellation of Reticulum. The star group is about 220 trillion miles from earth. The document mentioned a "Project Aquarius," which contained 16 volumes of information collected from the beginning of the U.S. Government's investigation of UFOs and Identified Alien Craft (IAC).

The project was originally established in 1953 by order of then President Eisenhower and under the control of the National Security Council and an organization called "MJ-12." In 1958, the U.S. Government recovered another alien aircraft from the desert of Utah. The IAC was in excellent flying condition and a technological marvel for the Air Force. However, the operating instrumentation of the craft was way beyond anything that our US scientists could understand. The IAC was stored in a Top Secret facility in Nevada which was the same facility I was at in July 1969 15 miles SE of Indian Springs.

In April 1964, two USAF intelligence officers met with members of an Extraterrestrial Biological Entity's (EBE's) alien race in the desert of New Mexico. The actual meeting occurred just west of Stallion Range, which is just north of Trinity. The meeting lasted two hours and communications between the AF intelligence personnel and the alien was conducted by sign language and eventually telepathy. The document finished with discussions of the continuing UFO investigations by the U.S. Government.

After reading the document, I was stunned and couldn't sleep for days. I would awake at night wondering if the aliens were just visiting Earth or preparing for an invasion; eventually I adjusted. I will go into more details later in the chapter.

As part of my job, I became involved with an official disclosure program starting in 1979 when the United States Government assigned me from one

68

Air Force agency to the role as a special investigator for UFO reports. It was my feeling at the time along with my colleagues that the government's information on UFOs and aliens should be presented and made largely availble to the public. There is only a small portion that we have gathered from the extraterrestrials that should be classified or safeguarded. I believe, that since we are in contact with extraterrestrials, that this information shouldn't be hidden from the public. Another part of my job was collecting raw UFO information in the field and analyzing that information. We then wrote reports and forwarded those reports to superiors in Washington, DC specifically, the CIA-DCI and Headquarters of the Air Force office of Special Investigations, Special Projects (AFOSI/PJ), who were our direct superiors.

There were a number of us (about 50 in sub units) assigned to Domestic Collections (Special Projects or PJ Office) of the Air Force Office of Special Investigations, which was not only in the United States, but throughout the world. There were two or three individuals that worked with me at differing times and at times there were more than three people.

The collection efforts were broken into four regions: The Northeast, Central, Northwest and Southwest region. They are not all located on military bases. One for example is located in Houston in conjunction with NASA. The others are in Seattle, Washington, and Plattsburg Air Force Base (now closed). Plattsburg was the only one on an Air Force base. The central region is located near Dayton, OH.

We learned in the early days of Project Blue Book, Grudge and Sign that we didn't always get the right information from eyewitnesses. So, we were out there before Blue Book closed in December 1969 (actually it was in 1968) conducting investigations covertly. After Blue Book was closed it was strictly covert. Our job in the field was to investigate sightings, landings, or contacts with UFOs or extraterrestrials, and in a way that we would not draw public attention. We were disguised or under the cover of military or other federal agencies while investigating UFO sightings. Dr. Hynek of Blue Book fame was very knowledgeable about the existence of MJ-12 and extraterrestrial contact.

In 1968, or sometime in the latter part of 1967, a certain group of people within the United States Government, known to some people as MJ-12, decided that Blue Book had served its purpose, and they were afraid at the time that if they continued with Project Blue Book some of the information or guarded secrets that the U.S. government obtained from the investigation of UFOs would leak out into the public domain. So they decided to end Project Blue Book with an investigation by the University of Colorado—the so-called Condon Report—which basically stated that there wasn't anything to UFO sightings or that there were some unexplained--about 2,000 of them--but everything had been explained over the past 19 or so years.

The government then decided to go completely underground with the investigation and that's when the remaining parts of Blue Book were transferred to other intelligence agencies. These agencies already had on going parallel domestic investigations of UFOs even before Blue Book closed as mentioned before. We then continued the investigation of UFO sightings and landings in an official capacity sanctioned by the government, but clandestinely–without the knowledge of the public-and, I must say, without the knowledge of a lot of government agencies.

I believed, as did my colleagues, that the public over the years since the beginning of the '50s had learned to distort the UFO information in the public domain. Also, the United States government was afraid that the public would panic if they knew the whole story as bits and pieces of intelligence-technological data leaked out, become distorted, causing further panic.

Everyone has a right to freedom of information, except what's exempted under certain paragraphs of Title 5 of the United States Code. But, the public would continue to ask for information, continue to pry into the investigations, and eventually they might harm the process the government was taking to obtain information from the aliens.

We would run the whole covert UFO collection operation just like any other intelligence operation. We would solicit either wittingly or unwittingly of associates or of "cooperating people" as we would call them. We would recruit these people just as an intelligence officer would recruit people in a foreign country to provide us with information on UFO sightings. When they would give us information about a sighting or a landing, we would use ourselves in a cover capacity, identifying ourselves as some other person. We have even used newspaper personnel, wittingly and unwittingly, and scientists or, we would pose as a scientist.

After the information was collected, as mentioned before, it was sent to the intelligence community within Washington, DC. It would go through the Director of Central Intelligence, DCI (CC to AFOSI/PJ) since he was the director of all the intelligence agencies within the United States Government or was until the advent of a National Intelligence Director. From there, it's filtered to the appropriate individuals for analysis and filing. How the information was classified depended on the nature of the report. If the information contained sightings with contacts, then normally that was classified at the Top Secret Code Word level.

MJ-12

MJ-12 is a group of individuals within the intelligence community of the United States that controls the access to the information regarding UFOs and was created by President Truman in the late '40s. Their job was to investigate and keep track of information pertaining to UFOs. Part of their job was scientific advancement, but I believe their primary purpose was to keep track of the information coming in on UFOs and to analyze that information scientifically in a way that would advance our technology.

MJ-12 policy making is implemented in military units around the world.

Within the infrastructure of MJ-12, there are witting and unwitting personnel performing the operational tasks. Some field personnel collected and gathered information pertaining to UFO sightings, but they didn't always know they were collecting information for MJ-12.

The President of the United States does not control MJ-12. MJ-12 is an entity within the government that provides policy regarding ET and UFO activities; policies are created by MJ-12 and then the president is advised of that policy. The president gives permission to implement that policy by signing classified Executive Orders.

The Navy has the primary operational responsibilities for field activities relating to the MJ-12 policies. Besides information going to the CIA, the same information gathered in the field, not necessarily by Navy personnel, is also transmitted to the Navy for analysis.

The Naval research activity responsible for the operational activities of the MJ-12 policy is headquartered at the Naval Observatory in Washington, DC.

The National Security Agency and Defense Intelligence Agency personnel are used to implement the policies of MJ-12.

There are government officials and elected officials who are automatically briefed as to the existence of the MJ-12 projects. These elected officials include, the President, the Vice-President, the Director of Central Intelligence, and the Director of the National Security Agency.

Grudge and Sign

Project Grudge and Project Sign were earlier public forms of Project Blue Book. They were official investigations of UFOs done by the Army Air Force and then the Air Force.

Project Aquarius

Project Aquarius is a general operation, but there are specific sections within Project Aquarius where the received information regarding UFOs is filtered to MJ-12. MJ-12 gets the most secret of the secret.. Project Aquarius consisted of some of the following sub programs:

1. TS/ORCON) PROJECT BANDO: (PROWORD: RISK) originally established in 1949. Its mission was to collect and evaluate medical information from the surviving Alien creature and the recovered Alien bodies. This Project medically examined EBE-1 and provided United States medical researchers with certain answers to the evolution theory (OPR: CIA) (Terminated in 1974).
2. (TS/ORCON) PROJECT SIGMA: (PROWORD: MIDNIGHT) originally established as part of Project Gleem in 1954. Became a

separate project in 1976. Its mission was to establish communication with Aliens. This Project met with positive success, when in 1959, the United States established primitive communications with the Aliens. On April 25, 1964, a USAF intelligence officer met two Aliens at a prearranged location in the desert of New Mexico [Editor's note: This was Stallion range, just north of the Trinity site in NM] The contact lasted for approximately three hours. Based on the Alien's language given to us by EBE, the Air Force officer managed to exchange basic information with the two Aliens. This project is continuing at an Air Force base in New Mexico (OPR: MJ12/NSA).

3. (TS/ORCON) PROJECT SNOWBIRD: (PROWORD: CETUS) originally established in 1972. Its mission was to test fly a recovered alien aircraft. This project is continuing in Nevada (OPR: USAF/NSA/CIA/MJ12).

4. (TS/ORCON) PROJECT POUNCE: (PROWORD: DIXIE) originally established in 1968. Its mission was to evaluate all UFO/IAC information pertaining to space technology. PROJECT POUNCE continues (OPR: NASA/USAF).

As for presidents who knew, Bill Clinton and Ronald Reagan were briefed on the subject of UFOs and the historical aspects of it starting from the early days of the late '40s-early '50s. President Carter, former Presidents Ford, and Bush and Nixon had all been briefed. All of the presidents were told the top-secret results and not just a generalized: "Look, we're looking into this situation."

Public Deception

There are times when you deceive the public and you are doing the public a great service, and I certainly would protect the public with deception operations if it were for their own good. But, some aspects of these UFO investigations that have occurred over the years should not be withheld from the public. The general knowledge that there were aliens who landed on Earth back in the late '40s-- early '50s, and that we have had some type of crude communication with them, should not be kept from the public. My colleagues and I decided that this was the time (1983–1988) to come forward with information and try to present it in a noteworthy fashion in order for the public to be informed on this subject. The public was to be presented with the general knowledge that the United States had investigated UFO sightings, not only in the '50s-'90s to the present day, but that we are presently keeping track of visitations to this planet by aliens and their spacecraft.

Roswell, EBE-1

In July 1947, a spacecraft crashed in New Mexico and one alien was recovered alive, EBE-1. He was kept at Los Alamos after the July 1947 Roswell crash. He was interviewed or interrogated so to speak. It took over a year or so before the military intelligence people were able to communicate with him. The methods they used were not made clear. But once they were able to communicate with him he told them the basics of his knowledge and of the alien's knowledge in the exploration of planet Earth. His knowledge was not complete because he was basically a mechanic although he knew what he was taught and what he had learned. He certainly did not know it all and that was the impression and consensus of the intelligence personnel were investigating and interrogating him. He said he came from the Zeta Reticuli Star System, two suns together (~10th of a light year apart) or a co-moving wide binary system comprised of Zeta 1 and 2. EBE-1 came from the fourth planet of Zeta 2 called "Sieu" as mentioned earlier and having a period year of 432 days. From current information Sieu appears to be planet SERPO (see reference 1a and page 189).

Figure 1: EBE-1 likeness; Courtesy of Linda Howe's copy of an identical Eben drawing which matched Rick Doty's EBE-1 drawing.

The story that EBE-1 told was astonishing regarding his particular planet. This was obvious to both the military and scientific investigators that, culturally and technologically, EBE-1's planet was many thousands of years ahead of us. EBE-1 said they have been able to navigate the solar system in spacecraft for many thousands of years, and they have been exploring planet Earth since some 25,000 years ago. Between that time and 5,000 years ago, they populated the earth with a "human helper" in an area now called Mongolia.

Over a period of time, they placed "human helpers" throughout our planet, either in colonies or as individuals.

This information came from what is known as the "Bible" or "Yellow Book" within the intelligence community. The "Yellow Book" is the alien's history of the universe.

Another book, called the "Red Book," is a very, very thick detailed account summary of the investigations that have been conducted from 1947 to the present with updates every 5 years containing nothing but official information. This orange-brown book contains everything that occurred during the Truman years up through the three aliens being guests of the U.S. Government. It contains technological data gathered from the aliens, medical, and autopsy data gathered from the dead aliens found in the desert (Roswell and other crash sites). Also contained is information obtained from the extraterrestrials regarding their social structure and information pertaining to their views of the universe. The 1977 Carter briefing document came from this "Red Book."

Captured UFOs

Besides what others and I observed at Wright-Patterson AFB, Indian Springs, Area 51-S4 and other places, that even with a very high security clearance, you couldn't get close to captured UFOs. The one UFO I saw was up on a platform. It was a circular-shaped object or disc shaped and it had an opening on one side with a battery of lights on the top. I got perhaps within a 150 yards of it. That was in the early 1980s.

EBE-2 and 3

There is a closed circuit/videotape interview of an alien (EBE-2, Figure 2) that was an exchange guest here starting from 1964 until 1984. An AF Colonel did the interview. I attended that interview (see Section 3, Chapter 2). From EBE-2, we learned a great deal of information about their race, culture and spacecraft. A third alien, EBE-3 was part of the same exchange program starting in 1978 or '79, '84 until 1989 or '93.

Figure 2: Looks very similar to EBE-2.

It was not until 1951- 52 sometime after the first alien was recovered (EBE-1), that a doctor devised a way of implanting a device in the throat of this alien. The alien quickly learned to verbalize English words and was able to speak using this new device.

The second alien (EBE-2) that came here had a device implanted into his throat, which enabled him to verbalize English words, although the words were not always recognizable.

Quarters?

The extraterrestrials, who are guests of the US government, reside in a number of different quarters around the US. They have one in New Mexico that is a simple apartment-style. The alien I'm familiar with eats a restricted diet; they don't seem to require fluids like we do. Their physiological structure enables them to absorb fluid from food, therefore they drink very little. They like and do eat vegetables. Their favorite snack is ice cream, especially strawberry. Their physiology structure differs from humans. They have a very simple digestive system. Their heart and lung, or equivalent of a heart and lung, is one organ or all connected which will be discussed under the anatomy of the aliens.

The apartments these aliens are put in are all located in secure areas with the exception of one (EBE female, that's what all the Bird Code was about, see Addendum) in Washington, DC. The apartment in New Mexico is located within a restricted area; in fact, it is actually a restricted area within a restricted area.

These aliens enjoy all types of music, but especially Tibetan music, which we understand, is similar to their music. They like a particular style of Tibetan music played by traditional Tibetan instruments like Indian style music.

Disclosure

"Operation White " was one of the many official government programs for public disclosure and "The Day the Earth Stood Still" is an example of how Hollywood was used to get the message out. Other operations were:

Red Snow; Long Silver; Kit Kleen; Silver Steam; Sandal Leg; Walrus; Seven Doors; Seven Princes; Seven Kings; Seven Lights; Seven Pawns; Pawns Right; Pawns Up; Dragger Kings; Dragger Prince; Dragger Lane; Lance Rite; Lance Green; Lance Red; Gallant Horse; Gallant Kings; Gallant Prince; Tight End.

These are only the ones I can remember. As the reader can see, I worked on many different operations or programs. We had many different programs dealing with public disclosure or disinformation operations against a public entity.

Communications

The National Security Agency has devised a communications system to communicate with the aliens. It's some type of electronic binary pulse. Recent frequencies reportedly used were, 274.750, 377.550 and 310.920 MHZ. The communications takes place between the Earth and the alien ships. There are reportedly receiving points in Nevada and California. The communications are translated by a computer, which gives the landing coordinates to the National Security Agency, so we know the location of the landing and the purpose, i.e., collect resources for their spacecraft or to have verbal contact.

Unknown Landings

We investigated unknown landings or the ones the aliens were not telling us about. Why they are landing at these undisclosed locations is a mystery to the US government (Is it related to the reported abductions?); the majority of undisclosed landings are in remote areas away from towns. Examples are southern and central New Mexico, central California, the desert area of southern California, Nevada, Utah and northern areas of the US such as Montana and South Dakota. As to why they only make contact with certain scientists and government officials and not the general public can only be speculated on. The best guess is, and as difficult as it may sound to us, they are so far advanced that they cannot communicate with us the way we communicate with each other on this planet. Perhaps that is a result of them being scared. A corollary to this is described in interviews of EBE-1 in 1949 and '50 where EBE-1 was described as extremely scared of not just being in a strange place, but of us as a different type of creature.

Physical Conditions, Characteristics and Anatomy of the Aliens

They live approximately 350 to 400 Earth years and can travel from their planet in the Zeta Reticuli Star System to our planet in approximately 90 days (this was later reduced to 30 days). The distance to Earth is approximately 39 light years. The alien's form of travel is by spacecraft, but they seem to use a form of physics that we don't understand. They seem to bend the distance between Earth and their planet in traveling, which shortens the duration of travel (2). The aliens have a mother ship, which orbits earth, and then have smaller explorer ships which actually land on the earth. These explorer ships are saucer shaped between 30-50 feet in diameter and have a crew of between 3 and 10 aliens.

The medical examinations from the "Red Book" describe these aliens as creatures 3'4" to 3'8" tall (Figures 3-6 next page). Their eyes are extremely large, almost insect like. Their eyes have a couple of different inner lids and that's probably because they were born on a planet whose sun had a high ultraviolet output. They have just 2 openings where their nose would be. They have a small mouth. They either have no teeth (hard gum-like area) or flat teeth for chewing vegetables. They have four fingers without thumbs with webbing between the fingers. Their feet are small and web like. They wear clothing similar to us, but they apparently don't require the type of clothing that we would require. Their society and culture are different than ours.

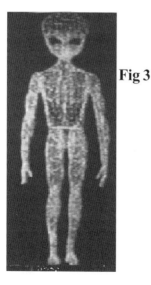

Fig 3

Fig 4

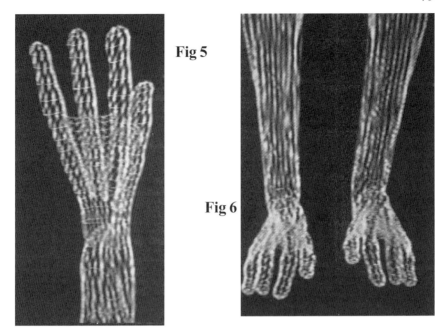

Fig 5

Fig 6

Their internal organs are quite simple (Figures 7-8). They have a one organ, which encompasses what we would refer to as heart and lungs. It's one pulmonary sac, which does the job of our heart and lungs. The digestive system is really simple (Figure 8).

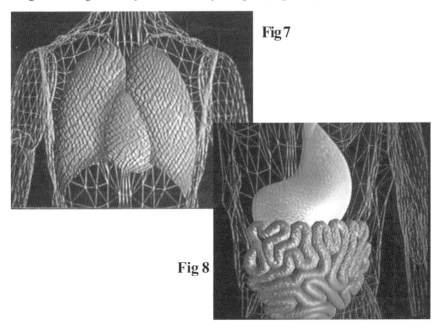

Fig 7

Fig 8

They only have liquid wastes and not solid waste; they transfer all the food they eat into liquids. Their bodies extract the liquid out of the food, but they can eat some basic food products like the vegetables and fruit that we eat. They have problems digesting meat products or they don't eat meat on their planet.

Their skin structure is extremely elastic and hard; probably hardened from their sun.

Their brain is more complex than ours; it has several more different lobes than ours. Their eyes are controlled by the front of their brain where in humans it is the back of the brain (Figure 9).

Their hearing is quite better than ours (Figure 9) and almost better than a dog's; they have small areas on the sides of their head that function as ears. They have males and females, and their females have sexual organs similar to our females but there are

Fig 9

some differences in the ovary system. Their kidney and bladder is one organ (Figure 10). They excrete waste, and they have another organ that transfers the solid waste into liquid wastes.

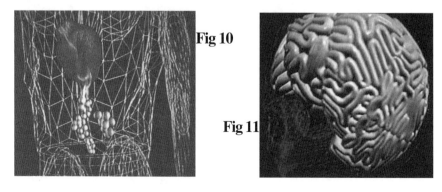

Fig 10

Fig 11

The aliens have an average IQ of over 200 and an average brain size of 1800 cc (Figure 11) versus humans with ~ 1350-1400 cc. They can regulate their IQ according to the culture they are in contact with. Supposedly, if they are visiting a primitive planet, they can "lower their IQ" in order to communicate with the culture.

More Than One Species

We have reason to believe that there is more than one species visiting earth. In the past 10 years and more, there have been a number of sightings, landings and contacts with an alien that was quite different than the Ebens (nick name for Extraterrestrial Biological Entities), who are small. These other aliens are larger and have hair whereas the typical gray Eben has no hair on their bodies. These creatures were blonde-like. They had hair and were relatively tall compared to the other Ebens or almost five feet according to some recent sighting reports. The domestic collection people within the intelligence community investigated many of these cases which gave them the knowledge that there were other aliens or at least one other alien race visiting this planet. One of the MJ-12 members indicated that there are nine (9) different species of aliens visiting this planet.

Security

All the above information is/was very closely guarded: Only people with a "need-to-know" have access to the information (SCI). It's compartmented or specially-compartmented information. But over the years, I know of some people who have had access to the program. The presidents I knew had access and Mr. Poindexter, who was head of the Defense Intelligence Agency and now head of DARP's "Total Awareness" Program until recently. Admiral Bobby Ray Inman, who was a former Deputy Director of the Defense Intelligence Agency and former Deputy Director of the Central Intelligence Agency, had partial or complete knowledge of the UFO subject. Secretary of Defense Brown during the Carter Administration, and earlier Secretary of Energy Schlesinger had access to the information.

The government can keep a secret this long by a number of means. One being, compartmenting the data within the government, or the intelligence community, or they can run deception operations, deceiving the public, or deceiving private UFO groups. They present the groups with faulty information, unbelievable data, which in turn, the groups publish, and are then ridiculed. That misinforms the public, and keeps the government information compartmentalized and protected.

Contact

The whole contact with the aliens terminated after EBE-1 died in the early '50s. He died of an unknown disease and our doctors and medical personnel had no idea why he died. Later in 1959 or 1960 we started receiving some communications from some place in the universe but we had no idea where it was coming from. Over a period of time, this information was translated to a particular point on the planet or certain coordinates. In April 1964 (Stallion range near Trinity mentioned before), two Air Force intelligence officers went to that particular location where a landing was agreed on and they had a face-to-face encounter with aliens. "Close Encounters of the Third Kind" was based on this actual event. The United States is the primary country maintaining contact with the aliens.

Presently, the extraterrestrials who have contact with the U.S. government have a base in Nevada. These ETs have complete control over this base. Ernie said this in Chapter 1 of Section 1.

Russia, based on our intelligence collection, has had a number of alien contacts. In fact, UFO sightings within Russia between 1972 and 1982 were almost double that of the United States. The Russians have had contact since the early 50s.

Weapons

Recovered UFOs, to the best of my knowledge, didn't have any offensive onboard weapons systems but rather a defensive system that could cause electronic interference; it's not an offensive weapon. As a defensive system, it would cause electronic interference to any incoming aircraft or missiles.

Earlier in the 1950s, there had been some cases where Air Force jets had chased aliens and the jet crashed. There was reason to believe that it wasn't anything intentional on the part of the aliens. The aliens were probably just as mystified as we were, and therefore they made some type of defensive gesture on their part that caused our aircraft to be destroyed.

God

They have a universal religion and the simplest way to state it is that they believe in the universe as a supreme being rather than a supreme being creating the universe. One of the volumes of Project Aquarius has 30--40 pages devoted to details of their belief in a Deity.

The Yellow Book

I mentioned the Yellow Book earlier in this chapter, but I'd like to add that this book was brought by EBE-2 in April 1964 at the time of the Holloman landing (meaning Stallion range near Trinity). The book relates to the alien's planet, solar system, suns, culture, the societal makeup on the planet, the social structure of the aliens, and the alien's life among the earthlings. The original draft of the book was written in the alien's own language, but EBE-2 translated the book into English. As for humans, it would take a lifetime to read the book and another lifetime to understand it.

Crystal

The most intriguing in my experience with aliens is a crystal--an octagon-shaped crystal--which when held in the alien's hand, and viewed by a second person, displayed pictures. These pictures could be of the alien's home planet or of the earth thousands of years ago. The crystal always intrigued me, but I don't understand how it operates, nor do I think the government understands how it operates. I have seen the crystal, but I have not seen the pictures. The alien has control over the photographs. The alien must be holding the crystal in order for the pictures to appear. A colleague of mine has seen the crystal and a presentation of the pictures by the alien.

The Cash-Landrum Case

In the Cash-Landrum incident, military pilots piloted the craft. The craft represented one of many attempts by the U.S. government at reverse engineering of Alien craft. Helicopters were following the craft because the craft was experiencing severe control problems and it was thought by the U.S. crew that the craft was going to crash. In that case the craft didn't crash (Section 3, Chapter 3).

The Manzano Weapons Storage Area UFO Incident of August 1980

On the morning of August 11, 1980 (documents in Figures 12 and 13), a security advisr for Sandia National Laboratories informed me of the following incident. "On August 9, 1980, a Sandia security Guard reported that at approximately 12:20 a.m. he was driving east on Coyote Canyon access road on a routine building check of an alarmed structure. Sandia Laboratories owned several buildings in the Coyote Canton area. As the guard approached the structure he observed a bright light near the ground behind the structure. He first thought the object was a helicopter. But, after moving closer the guard observed a round dish-shaped object. He attempted to radio for a back-up patrol, but his vehicle radio wouldn't work. As he approached the object on foot armed with a shotgun the object took off in a vertical direction at a high rate of speed. The guard, a former helicopter mechanic in the Army, stated that the object was not a helicopter." After receiving this information I briefed the commander. I was then instructed to make a report, classify it "Secret" and forward the message to Headquarters Air Force Office of Special Investigations (PJ), Washington, DC.

On September second, 1980 the Commander of the 1608th Security Police Squadron, Manzano Base and Kirtland AFB related the following: "On August 8th 1980 three Security Policemen assigned to his squadron while on duty inside Manzano Weapons Storage Area sighted a UFO in the skies over Coyote Canyon (Figure 12)." This sighting corresponded to the sighting made by the Sandia Security Guard. Because of this sighting base officials were extremely interested in the activity over Coyote Canyon. I completed an

COMPLAINT FORM

HA 1 V 25

ADMINISTRATIVE DATA		

TITLE	DATE	TIME
KIRTLAND AFB, NM, 8 Aug – 3 Sep 80, Alleged Sigthings of Unidentified Aerial Lights in Restricted Test Range.	2 – 9 Sept 80	1200
	PLACE	
	AFOSI Det 1700, Kirtland AFB, NM	

	HOW RECEIVED	
X IN PERSON	TELEPHONICALLY	IN WRITING

SOURCE AND EVALUATION

MAJOR ERNEST E. EDWARDS

RESIDENCE OR BUSINESS ADDRESS	PHONE
Commander, 1608 SPS, Manzano Kirtland AFB, NM	4-7516

CR __44__ APPLIES

II	SUMMARY OF INFORMATION

REMARKS

1. On 2 Sept 80, SOURCE related on 8 Aug 80, three Security Policemen assigned to 1608 SPS, KAFB, NM, on duty inside the Manzano Weapons Storage Area sighted an unidentified light in the air that traveled from North to South over the Coyote Canyon area of the Department of Defense Restricted Test Range on KAFB, NM. The Security Policemen identified as: SSGT STEPHEN FERENZ, Area Supervisor, AIC MARTIN W. RIST and AMN ANTHONY D. FRAZIER, were later interviewed separately by SOURCE and all three related the same statement: At approximately 2350hrs., while on duty in Charlie Sector, East Side of Manzano, the three observed a very bright light in the sky approximately 3 miles North-North East of their position. The light traveled with great speed and stopped suddenly in the sky over Coyote Canyon. The three first thought the object was a helicopter, however, after observing the strange aerial maneuvers (stop and go), they felt a helicopter couldn't have performed such skills. The light landed in the Coyote Canyon area. Sometime later, three witnessed the light take off and leave proceeding straight up at a hight speed and disappear.

2. Central Security Control (CSC) inside Manzano, contacted Sandia Security, who conducts frequent building checks on two alarmed structures in the area. They advised that a patrol was already in the area and would investigate.

3. On 11 Aug 80, RUSS CURTIS, Sandia Security, advised that on 9 Aug 80, a Sandia Security Guard, (who wishes his name not be divulged for fear of harassment), related the following: At approximately 0020hrs., he was driving East on the Coyote Canyon access road on a routine building check of an alarmed structure . As he approached the structure he observed a bright light near the ground behind the structure. He also observed an object he first thought was a helicopter. But after driving closer, he observed a round disk shaped object. He attempted to radio for a back up patrol but his radio would not work. As he approached the object on foot armed with a shotgun, the object took off in a vertical direction at a high rate of speed. The guard was a former helicopter mechanic in the U.S. Army and stated the object he observed was not a helicopter.

4. SOURCE advised on 22 Aug 80, three other security policemen observed the same

DATE FORWARDED HQ AFOSI	10 Aug 80	AFOSI FORM 88 ATTACHED	☐ YES	☐ NO

DATE	TYPED OR PRINTED NAME OF SPECIAL AGENT	SIGNATURE
8 Sept 80	RICHARD C. DOTY, SA	

DISTRICT FILE NO.	DCII RESULTS	
80 1 7 8 9 3 - 0/22	☐ NEGATIVE	☐ POSITIVE (See Attached)

AFOSI FORM 1 JUN 76   PREVIOUS EDITION WILL BE USED

Figure 12a: OSI Complaint form

86

aerial phenomena described by the first three. Again the object landed in Coyote Canyon. They did not see the object take off.

5. Coyote Canyon is part of a large   restricted test range used by the Air Force Weapons Laboratory, Sandia Laboratories, Defense Nuclear Agency and the Department of Energy. The range was formerly patrolled by Sandia Security, however, they only conduct building checks there now.

6. On 10 Aug 80, a New Mexico State Patrolman sighted avaerial object land in the Manzano's between Belen and Albuquerque, NM. The Patrolman reported the sighting to the Kirtland AFB Command Post, who later referred the patrolman to the AFOSI Dist 17. AFOSI Dist 17 advised the patrolman to make a report through his own agency. On 11 Aug 80, the Kirtland Public Information office advised the patrolman the USAF no longer investigates such sightings unless they occured on an USAF base.

7. WRITER contacted all the agencies who utilized the test range and it was learned no aerial tests are conducted in the Coyote Canyon area. Only ground tests are conducted.

8. On 8 Sept 80, WRITER learned from Sandia Security that another Security Guard observed a object land near an alarmed structure sometime during the first week of August, but did not report it until just recently for fear of harassment.

9. The two alarmed structures located within the area contains HQ CR 44 material.

Figure 12b: OSI Complaint form continued

MULTIPURPOSE INTERNAL OSI FORM
(Complete only applicable items)

LG NO.(S) 17/1V0	SUBJECT	FILE NO.
GET NO (S)	KIRTLAND AFB, NM, 8 Aug - 3 Sep 80	8017D93-0/29
HEADQUARTERS	Alleged Sightings of Unidentified Aerial	TRANSMITTAL DATE
(w) NO 17/BID	Lights in Restricted Test Range	28 Oct 80
GET NO		SUSPENSE DATE
HEADQUARTERS		

REFERENCE

AFOSI Fm 1, 8 Sep 80, Same Title

MINOR DISCREPANCIES NOTED ARE LISTED BELOW

YOUR DISTRICT IS DESIGNATED OFFICE OF ORIGIN

ATTACHED REQUIRES INVESTIGATION IN YOUR AREA

DETERMINE SUBJECT'S ACCESS TO CLASSIFIED INFORMATION AS REQUIRED BY OSIM 124-1, PARA 2-6-3

FORWARD RESULTS DIRECTLY TO OFFICE OF ORIGIN, OR TO

NO FURTHER INVESTIGATION CONTEMPLATED

OUR FILES REFLECT PRIOR INVESTIGATION BY _____ DTD _____ FILE _____ (By copy of this form)

OUR FILES REFLECT PRIOR INVESTIGATION/SUMMARY ATTACHED

INVESTIGATION CONTINUING AND YOU WILL BE FURNISHED FURTHER REPORTS.

DISCONTINUE INVESTIGATION FORWARD RESULTS OF ANY INVESTIGATION ACCOMPLISHED.

DISCREPANCIES BETWEEN LEAD REQUEST AND DEVELOPED INFORMATION ARE SET FORTH.

REPORT OF COMMAND ACTION HAS NOT BEEN RECEIVED

REQUEST STATUS OF THIS MATTER AND OR DATE REPORT MAY BE EXPECTED. *(Requester, forward-2 copies of this form.) (Recipient, use one received copy for answer with proper signature in remarks section unless OSI directives state reply not required.)*

REFER ATTACHED TO INTERESTED COMMANDER FOR INFORMATION OR ACTION IF NOT PREVIOUSLY REPORTED

CHECK WORLD WIDE LOCATOR FOR BELOW LISTED PERSON OR SUBJECT

ATTACHED IS FORWARDED FOR INFORMATION AND/OR ACTION

UPON REMOVAL OF ATTACHMENT(S):   THE CLASSIFICATION ON THIS CORRESPONDENCE WILL BE
☐ RETAINED. ☐ DOWNGRADED TO _____   ☐ CANCELED. ☐ MARKED "FOR OFFICIAL USE ONLY."

(If classification is retained, with or without attachments, indicate reason for security classification and grouping per APR 205-1.)

REMARKS

On 24 Oct 80, Dr PAUL FREDRICK BENNEWITZ, Male Born 30 Sep 27, KS, Civ, SSAN: [b7C]
[b7C] Albuquerque, NM, contacted SA RICHARD C. DOTY through Major
ERNEST E. EDWARDS, Commander, 1608 SPS, Kirtland AFB, NM and related he had knowledge and
evidence of threats against Manzano Weapons Storage area. The threat was from Aerial
phenomena over Manzano.

On 26 Oct 80, SA DOTY, with the assistance of JERRY MILLER, GS-15, Chief, Scientific
Advisor for Air Force Test and Evaluation Center, KAFB, interviewed Dr. BENNEWITZ at his
home in the Four Hills Section of Albuquerque, which is adjacent to the northern boundary
of Manzano Base. (NOTE: MILLER is a former Project Blue Book USAF Investigator who was
assigned to Wright-Patterson AFB W-PAFB, OH, with FTD. Mr. MILLER in one of the most knowledgeable and impartial investigators of Aerial Objects in the southwest). Dr. BENNEWITZ
produced photographs and over 2600 feet of 8mm. motion picture film depicting unidentified
aerial objects flying over and around Manzano Weapons Storage Area and Coyote Canyon Test
area. Dr. BENNEWITZ has been conducting independent research into Aerial Phenomena for
the last 15 months. Dr. BENNEWITZ also produced several electronic recording tapes.

COPIES TO	ATTACHMENTS	FILE STAMP AND/OR OTHER
Q AFOSI/IVOS; File		9017D93-0/29×1
NAME, GRADE, TITLE, SIGNATURE		
THOMAS A. CSEH, Major, USAF		
Commander		
Base Investigative Detachment	FOR OFFICIAL USE ONLY	

OSI FORM 96
JAN 74

Figure 13a: Internal AFOSI form

allegedly showing high periods of electrical magnetism being emitted from Manzano/Coyote Canyon area. Dr. BENNEWITZ also produced several photographs of flying objects taken over the general Albuquerque area. He has several pieces of electronic surveillance equipment pointed at Manzano and is attempting to record high frequency electrical beam pulses. Dr. BENNEWITZ claims these Aerial Objects produce these pulses.

3. After analyzing the data collected by Dr. BENNEWITZ, Mr MILLER related the evidence clearly shows that some type of unidentified aerial objects were caught on film; however, no conclusions could be made whether these objects pose a threat to Manzano/Coyote Canyon areas. Mr MILLER felt the electronical recording tapes were inconclusive and could have been gathered from several conventional sources. No sightings, other than these, have been reported in the area.

4. Mr MILLER has contacted FTD personnel at W-P AFB, OH, who expressed an interest and are scheduled to inspect Dr. BENNEWITZ' data.

5. Request a DCII check be made on Dr BENNEWITZ.

6. This is responsive to HQ CR 44.

7. Command was briefed but did not request an investigation at this time.

Figure 13b: Internal AFOSI form continued

AFOSI Form 1, Complaint Form (Figure 13), documenting my initial investigation and forwarded it to OSI headquarters. A few days after OSI headquarters received the report, two OSI agents from the Special Projects Branch of the AFOSI (PJ) (Special Projects) arrived on base. They began an investigation into the sightings. Shortly after their arrival, three employees of the National Security Agency (NSA) arrived at Kirtland to conduct the follow-up investigation into the sightings. I worked closely with these individuals (both NSA and PJ). After a month at Kirtland, both agencies PJ and NSA concluded the sightings were legitimate and worth further analysis. Both the NSA and PJ agents made a detailed report. I saw a draft of this report in November 1980, but that was the last and only time.

Two years later while at headquarters OSI, I asked to see a copy of the report but was told it was not available. Later, I talked to one of the PJ agents who investigated the incident at Kirtland. I asked him to see a copy of the report he had filed. He was told that NSA took his report and he has not seen it since.

In October 1980, during the investigation of the Coyote Canyon sightings, a NSA agent advised that a Paul Bennewitz who resided in the Four Hills Housing Area directly north of Manzano Base outside the perimeter was directing electronic signals toward Manzano Base. The NSA agent asked me to check into Bennewitz's activity. I did some preliminary investigation and determined that Paul Bennewitz was a friend of the commander of the 1608th Security Police Squadron, the original source of the sightings over Coyote Canyon. I asked the commander to speak to Bennewitz and find out what he was up to. This way Bennewitz would think the commander (his friend) was making inquiries instead of the NSA. NSA wanted to stay out of the initial contact with Bennewitz. The commander spoke with Bennewitz and obtained the basic information regarding Bennewitz's research. When I briefed headquarters on Bennewitz, they immediately wanted me to visit Mr. Bennewitz's home, take photographs and determine whether further investigation of Bennewitz was warranted. Headquarters, specifically the PJ branch, suggested I take along UFO expert Jerry Miller. Miller was a staff intelligence officer with the Air Force Operation Test and Evaluation Center (AFOTEC), Kirtland AFB. Miller was a former Project Blue Book investigator. I had met Mr. Miller earlier in

1980 during a special security briefing. Miller had a vast amount of knowledge regarding UFOs. Since headquarters suggested that I use Miller, I assumed that Miller was well known throughout the intelligence community.

On October 26th 1980, Miller and I visited Bennewitz at his home. Bennewitz showed some film of aerial objects flying over and around Manzano and still photographs of UFOs filmed over northern New Mexico. We viewed electronic equipment at Bennewitz's house, which was aimed at Manzano. I covertly photographed all his equipment including some of his still photographs. I also photographed the interior of Bennewitz's home at the request of NSA. I assumed that NSA had further plans for Bennewitz. The meeting we had was just one of many over the next year.

After analyzing the material information obtained from Bennewitz, base officials became very interested. The base commander and the Director of the Air Force Weapons Laboratory wanted a meeting with Bennewitz which occurred on November 10th 1980. The meeting, which was taped recorded, was attended by a number of base officials and scientific personnel. After the meeting, several base officials decided to continue an independent scientific investigation of Bennewitz to analyze the information he presented. I was not privy to that investigation since it involved purely scientific personnel. To this day, I have no knowledge of what the scientific investigation disclosed. For a recent book on this case see (3). The book is a mix of truth with a number of distortions but fun reading.

New Paris Ohio Case of 1989 & 1993

In the spring of 1993, I assisted in the evaluation of tape recordings which involved a reported Alien abduction case in New Paris, OH. By this time, I had been long retired from the Air Force, but having never lost contact with my LANL sources, we were able to set up a testing session. This involved an LANL contractor assisted by a sub-contractor. There was another person named "Raven. " This is the same Raven that Jaime Shandera talks about in the Raven Addendum. The evaluation was performed on tape recordings made in 1989 as well as in 1993. What follows is a synopsis of what was analyzed.

Bizarre metallic phone recordings made in the winter/spring of 1989 and the spring of 1993. All of the recordings were made by Connie Fisher or Robert Collins. Recordings were made using either a regular or micro-cassette recorder.

Both a government acoustics contractor and government acoustics expert sat down, listened, and then evaluated the tapes. Then they gave their independent analysis and compared notes. Here is a synopsis of what they found:

1) Sounds generated then transmitted; sounds not generated by phone; sounds came through a phone line, all sounds were machine generated.

2) Robert Collins did not generate those sounds.

3) Connie's true voice was her true voice. The "other" Connie voice was a reverb machine voice. When they filtered out the "reverb voice" the voices were the same. Voiceprints from the two tapes showed similar voices or same voice.

4) Those death threats were made on a tape recorder and then put through a reverb then played through the phone. You could hear the click of the tape as it was going on and off. Age of male person on tape was estimated to be 25-30 years, more than likely having a white-Anglo background.

Robert Collins said he had received a phone call from a voice that sounded like Connie's. This voice told him that "they," meaning the contractor and acoustics expert, wouldn't find anything; that they wouldn't be able to prove or demonstrate any differences between Connie's real voice and the "machine voice."

After all of the discussion and not wanting to dismiss the case, Raven said he would like the following from Robert Collins and/or Connie:

1) Need at least a 30-minute covertly recorded conversation either on the phone or in person of Connie talking about these aliens; needed this to do a

voice stress test. Robert told me that he had already covertly recorded a 30 minute conversation with Connie. Later, he sent a copy of the tape to me which I sent on. In the end, I never heard back from the contractor or Raven about the tape I had forwarded to them.

2) To obtain either fingernail or blood samples from Connie for a DNA check. From that, Raven said they could determine a thousand different things or whether she had been altered or not. That statement got me wondering how much Raven really knew.

Raven made a cryptic comment that some years ago humans and the aliens had done some experiments using human and alien tissue samples, but wouldn't go into details with me. For a further discussion of this hear Rick Doty and Robert Collins' phone conversation on the New Paris Ohio case: http://www.ufoconspiracy.com/reports/doty-collins-phonechat.htm.

Metallic Voices? Below are links to some of the phone recordings made during the New Paris case: http://www.ufoconspiracy.com/misc/new-paris.mp3 and, http://ww.ufoconspiracy.com/misc/new-paris-rmc.mp3.

Finally, since retiring from the Air Force in November 1988, I have managed to have a successful second career as a New Mexico State Trooper having received many commendations for my outstanding work in the field of law enforcement. During the last few years, I was able to finish my law degree with an online school (editor: no verification of this) and plan to take the New Mexico State Bar exam at some future date. From the early 1990s to present I did consulting work for both the Fox Network's "X-Files" and Steven Spielberg's "Taken" mini series which appeared on the Science Fiction channel during December 2002.

I certainly do not want to end the story here so let's move to a more sinister subject in Chapter 5 which fits neatly into UFO mythology and folklore.

ADDENDUM

QUOTH THE RAVEN NARRATIVE

The Wilderness of Mirrors —James Jesus Angleton

Jaime Shandera writes (4): When Raven came into the UFO disclosure picture in 1991, he seemed to be laying out a scenario that was to make the information palatable for public consumption. Of course, the nature of the discussion is, unfortunately, never palatable in some camps. In the initial briefing during the first meeting with Raven, a number of things were revealed. Raven, as we were told, was very involved with MJ-12 and can't surface. He had been involved for over 30 years and worked "out" of Los Alamos National Laboratory (LANL).

One of the first surprises from Raven was the existence of an Ultra Top Secret group called the OROCA Panel: A panel, which had been in existence since the '50s. The panel is above MJ-12 and meets at CIA headquarters in Langley, VA, in a SCIF (Sensitive Compartmented Information Facility) room underground at Level 3. The existence of this Level 3 itself is highly classified. In fact, it is bypassed when accessing other underground levels. Hawk (Ernie Kellerstrass) once stated that you begin to realize the existence of the inaccessible areas when you time the elevator rides between different levels as you go down. A discrepancy occurs in the greater distance between two levels, a discrepancy not readily noticeable to the casual observer.

Regarding Ernie Kellerstrass, in a taped phone conversation (1996) he mentions EBE-2 leaving in 1984 and EBE-3 (female) leaving in 1989. But, before EBE-3 left, she met with six (6) U.S. Senators, but there were no Senate names mentioned by Ernie. EBE-3 or some female EBE was the same EBE Jaime and Bill were set-up to meet and what all the Bird Code was about (see last two paragraphs in this addendum). Ernie also mentioned that we had 12 more humans ready for an exchange program departing on April 24th 1997 and that former President Ronald Reagan had a couple of meetings with both EBE-2 and 3 while he was president.

Continuing: When Raven began working in this area, he thought MJ-12 and OROCA were the same; he found out later they were not. The oldest OROCA documents he had seen were from 1951. The highly classified section of Los Alamos where Raven worked periodically had a series of underground levels and is known as the "Dulce Complex" or TA 49 at Los Alamos. The surface is level 1 (this entry was closed off a few years ago) and there are five (5) levels underground. The underground levels are not accessed by any single elevator shaft or stairwell. The levels are offset and not stacked in any normal concept of construction. The design makes accidental or hostile penetration virtually impossible. The design also makes sabotage or even a direct bomb hit incapable of destroying the facility, at least in the total. An age-old security system is in effect with color badges. The color of your badge indicates what level you can go to. The highest clearance will have all colors on the badge.

The subject of UFOs and related areas take up 70 percent of Raven's workweek. Raven stated that the aliens have provided many items of interest to us, but we are still trying to find ways to use them. He said there are two (2) craft in Nevada that have been provided by the aliens (see Doty comments). He said that the aliens were not responsible for our present STEALTH technology, that we developed it, and the Ebens (nick name for Extraterrestrial Biological Entities) used a cloaking effect, much like the Romulans in "Star Trek" do, which makes them invisible, but not amongst themselves.

When asked if the ETs were currently here, Raven said not for several years (big questions about this) as they come periodically. They did not trust Reagan and were last here in 1988. By that Raven meant a permanent presence here. We do have a way to communicate with them by a scattered binary hyper-burst. It sends a signal faster than the speed of light. "Heron" (Jerry Miller, now retired from civil service in the Air Force) was aware of NASA experimenting with it in its primitive stages. When asked what messages we send, he said, they were responses to questions the Ebens have posed to us.

Raven said he cannot and would not meet to talk to us, but he will see if there is some way to assist. He was well aware of our research and things we had written. He said he would not discuss details about the Ebens. When asked if there was a human-ET exchange program, he said, "They have been here, we have been there." He said that we know the alien races who are and will be here; there are no surprises. It continued to sound as though he was addressing things for public consumption avoiding sensitive issues and the present and putting emphasis on the past. He stated that there were different species of aliens, he was aware of every one, and when asked if we are in contact with different ones, he said no, only the ones who are here.

He went onto say that all this got started in the 1930s when U.S. Army intelligence was provided some information. The Roswell incident actually happened pretty much as stated. There was one live alien, while the others died. The live alien died after a few years and was picked up in 1964 during the Holloman AFB official contact. They asked for the return of EBE-1 so we gave him back. We still have the pictures and medical research for EBE-1. Blue Book was truthful as there were many unexplained sightings with the Ebens doing reconnaissance, exploration and mapping. They took some animals and some mutilations were allowed, but controlled (serious questions about the truthfulness of this).

Raven said that there are about 200 other intelligent, sentient species scattered through out the universe that the Ebens have identified and often times interacted with. The Ebens are about 20-25,000 years ahead of us; a very long time ago they had a war with another race that is now dominated by the Ebens.

Betty and Barney Hill were taken on board a craft. They *weren't* abducted, according to Raven. He was very defensive with his phrasing. Raven said they subconsciously volunteered. Thousands have been taken on board alien spacecraft. They have been examined, never killed, and then released. The abductees have dreams, a lot about souls, which are about souls in the universe. When we die, our souls travel around until they find a new "home" in a new physical body to animate. All this was apparently revealed by the aliens. They do not harm anyone during their abductions and they are now through with this examination process; the next phase is the intellect.

Raven's efforts here seem to confirm that something is going on with "alien abductions" (as they are popularly known), but nothing as extreme as what's being reported. He went on to say that they believe in a supreme God, as we believe, but they are more religious than us; it is embedded in their society. He says Ebens can take the form of human beings. They could not before, but they can now, for the purpose of infiltrating society to obtain certain types of information. Raven says they may want to be exposed. It is apparently the government not wanting them exposed—not the aliens holding back—as they have held back only as a courtesy to us, Raven said. When asked about Whitley Strieber, Raven said he had an encounter; that he was a conduit for something, but that it did not pan out.

For someone who was not going to talk about the Ebens, Raven had said a mouthful. Our assessment was that Raven was prepping us for a disclosure that was inevitable. In that process, he was selective and tended to adjust the information. It is not that any of it was wrong; it was just being "polished." The alien abduction area was going to be sensitive for the government to deal with, no matter what. Raven's position goes further than any we had ever heard from the inside. It is easier to accept than the out right denials we had come to expect in the past. So, was Raven actually telling the truth or is he spinning the reported alien abduction incidences for political reasons? There are all of these stories of "mean spirited" aliens and horrible probes in both books and the mainstream media—are they a distortion of the true activity and nature which is more benign? There does seem to be a general dislike and distrust of some individuals within the government for those doing books and films about abductions. The real distrust from the government side is directed not at the people claiming the experience, but at some of the prominent researchers who lack the proper medical license or psychological training while nurturing, confirming, and characterizing the events as "horrible" and "traumatic."

The next few months saw increased activity. More meetings were held with Raven. Parrot (Senator Claiborne Pell) and Crow (not identified) joined the "Aviary" and the numbers began to swell. A list of names to contact was given to Sparrow (unidentified but this is not Rick Doty). One of the names on the list ran a facility that was known and had a publicly known function. Sparrow was to use Raven's name to gain access to information when contacting this individual. Once a meeting was arranged, the individual said since Raven had also contacted him, he would be happy to talk to Sparrow. He was escorted into a private room, where an enlightening discussion ensued.

"You know the public position of what we do here."

"Yes."

"Well, that's what I do here 80 percent of the time. But, it's the other 20 percent that I'm here for. This is the only sending and receiving station for alien communications on the planet."

Comment: The ET Communications facility was reportedly located in the Manzano Weapons Storage Area Plant 3.

"Seriously?"

"Quite seriously"

"How does that work?"

"From the time a message is sent from here until we receive a response takes 22 days. It's not 11 up and 11 back. Our sending takes longer than theirs."

Sparrow was impressed since this was quite a find. The use of Raven's name opened doors. The push on our end now was for us to put together a production deal. We needed to structure a TV show that could accommodate the information we were getting. We were first asked to outline two programs starting with Roswell to begin laying the historical perspective of ET contact. In addition to the outline of the programs, we were to include a "wish list" of proof that we felt we needed for each show. We were told that if we structured the show that they would supply the proof. The outline was completed and sent off. The next steps were negotiations with a major production company. Negotiations seemed to be going well with one company until their greed exceeded our civil rights, we walked away. The second round of negotiations went much better and most elements were worked out for a contract between us. The contract was on the table, not signed, but with a few points still to negotiate.

The End Game that Failed: How Working with the Government Flopped in 1991

Raven set up a major meeting. They needed us to define who would be the project director on our end. I was the only one who was skilled in both television production (Jaime Shandera) and this intelligence game we had been playing for years. The meeting that Raven was convening would include people from Washington and a CIA contract agent from L.A. Sparrow was going to be at the meeting, but wanted me to fly into Albuquerque to be on standby in case he needed me. There was to be a complete discussion about the television program. Certain key players in the Bush Administration were briefed. An operation was underway to brief the heads of various agencies to gain their support for the kind of rumblings that someone was real serious about going public. When you're focused on what you want to tell, you don't always look at how the administration in place needs to have a game plan to deal with the public. Secretary of Defense Cheney (now the Vice President) reportedly said he was against disclosure. The administration had nothing to gain and the Pentagon would need an additional $20 million. They would need the money to handle the increased staff to deal with the flood of Freedom of Information Requests (FOIA). The phones would be ringing off the hook and it would disrupt their ability to function with a normal business flow, let alone a crisis.

It was clear that a lot of thought was being put into the impact that this would have on all fronts. Now we were hearing things we hadn't considered, but that seemed so logical and expected. Things now seemed to be on a fast track of high exposure that would be hard to back down from. President Bush I was being mentioned often, but always in "careful" terms; careful in the sense that Bush was only supposed to be marginally aware that an operation was underway to test the political climate for release of UFO information. That sounded more like plausible deniability than fact or, proposals, discourse and then deny. If the briefings were underway-- and all indications suggested they were --then they could only have proceeded with Bush's express approval. There were hard rules we learned about MJ-12 over the years and that was there was great consistency. MJ-12 autonomy from the President worked only for day-to-day functioning, political decisions, briefing agencies, and disclosure. Anything that would impact the public and/or the administration required a Presidential directive, and this was not the exception, but the imperative and rule.

The rumblings we heard had to do with the difficult adjustments going on with the briefings and attitudes of the participants. Raven and Parrot were carrying out the briefings. Parrot was very cynical about Hollywood as he felt they sensationalized too much and could not be trusted to stay on track and remain focused. Raven felt it was the way to go and was the best opportunity to reach the largest audience with the ability to tell the whole story from historical roots. At first, NASA was negative, but the President's Scientific Adviser was very much in favor which was a big plus.

As the major meeting approached, I prepared to fly to Albuquerque. I understood my role, which was to be on standby. When I arrived, I checked into a hotel near the airport since this was also close to Kirtland AFB where the main meeting was to be held. When the plane landed and taxied to the terminal, I saw one of the jets out of Andrews AFB, MD. The plane had "United States of America" painted across the fuselage, which was the ones those U.S. Senators and other Washington dignitaries used on official business. It was parked inside the Air Force base fence at the Kirtland terminal.

At the hotel, I waited until I received contact with approximate times provided. I would need to be on standby. Once I got the call, I got something to eat. My first briefing came by early evening. Sparrow had a pre-meeting with Heron (Jerry Miller) and Parrot (Senator Pell).

Raven took the Washington visitor to Los Alamos for a briefing. On the previous day, they had been to the ET communication center (Manzano Weapons Storage Area, Kirtland AFB, Alb, NM, Plant 3). Parrot did not go; indeed, he said he had never been there, but sees the readouts. Heron (Jerry Miller) referred to the CIA-LA contact as "Washington's Man in L.A." He has been in L.A. for a long time and is thoroughly familiar with the Hollywood community and all of its players.

The evening meeting had been pushed back to accommodate the Los Angeles briefing. Sparrow felt this was a huge operation and was sure that the entire cross coordinating with officials in Washington was going on. He didn't know what the OPR (Office of Primary Responsibility) was, but he saw all the signs. He had done the same before but never to this extent nor on this level. There was a vast difference this time as opposed to 1987 when those running the operation were just above him. When they went higher, they were shut down. This time it was coming from the top. Heron (Jerry Miller) said he had never seen an operation interface with the media on this subject—never. They knew that when things started to break, Washington would be flooded with phone calls with reporters wanting to know things. All bases would be covered so that all offices would know how to respond.

Heron then spoke of some of the devices the aliens have given us. There is a beam device that can detect nuclear warheads. If it scans areas in Russia, for example, it can tell if there are nuclear warheads and their size and explosive yield. There is also a box that, when opened, emits what looks like light rays, but they are not light. They can't be measured on a spectrometer. When you pass a crystal or prism through this beam pictures show up. There doesn't appear to be anything in the box to cause the beams. There are no harmful side effects from the beams. The box has been tested and examined and it remains baffling. Heron says there is a warehouse full of these types of things that the aliens have given us which we cannot figure out.

Following the preliminary briefing, I was on my own for several hours. The next meeting was to take place in a vault room on the base (Kirtland AFB, NM). It is in these rooms that the most sensitive subjects are discussed. In fact, there are some classifications of information where discourse between two people can only be conducted in a vault room. The vault room cannot be bugged. The walls, ceiling and floor are electronically treated and the hallways and buildings are secured at all times. No matter your clearance level, if you are not designated during an assigned use, you cannot be admitted. If a document is typed in a vault-- as certain levels of classification require --then the typewriter itself remains classified until the ribbon is removed.

It was close to 2 a.m. before I received the briefing from the main meeting. It was stipulated that they wanted television presented in a way that was appealing to the public; they didn't want a lot of special effects. Every re-creation must be factual. The reason for doing this, they explained, was to prepare the public for the future: We will be visited by ET. We will soon be able to see aliens in space with new astronomical equipment and they want the public to be prepared. The

Ebens are a non-hostile species, exploring the universe; they go about their lives and let us do the same. The only aircraft we have lost due to alien sightings have been from chasing the alien craft beyond the designed tolerance of the plane. We have no knowledge of any offensive weapons on their part.

They don't want any government bashing for keeping the alien presence secret since they had a long-range plan and many presidents didn't want to implement it. Eisenhower said no; Kennedy was iffy; Johnson said get that crap out of here; Nixon had Watergate; Carter was fascinated and wanted to know everything; Reagan was afraid to deal with it; Bush I was, well, opinionated; and later, Kissinger warned Clinton not to, and Bush II said no.

Our proposal was received very well. It was taken back to Washington. Certain people still had to get into place. That was understood to mean Robert Gates (the current Defense Secretary) had to complete the confirmation process for Director of Central Intelligence (DCI).

There was a lot of special information relative to how we were to deal with the government, the networks, briefings, changes, time frames, etc.... It was stated that the aliens might be back as early as 1993. We are not in constant contact; there is a window of two or three months in the year (this statement doesn't explain all the UFO sightings). There have been other aliens here, several species in the last 60-70 years. One group was hostile, but not known to have harmed anyone; perhaps it was they who had carried out some of the alien abductions, but the Ebens will reportedly protect and shield us.

It was said that General Scrowcroft asked to be read into the program the moment he became National Security Adviser. He wanted to see the project manager (that was Raven) and asked like a child, "May I see something please?"

Following the meeting, I caught a couple hours of sleep and was on the first flight back to L.A. It certainly would appear that we were on the line in postcard number 2 that said, "The scene was set: The curtain to rise when the T-I-M-E was ripe." The scene was set like no other time in this long adventure. But, we still did not know what T-I-M-E meant. Hopefully, that wouldn't be another mountain to climb.

Almost immediately after I returned, a major problem began to erupt on our landscape. With the Gates hearing just days away, his role in the

Iran-Contra affair suddenly loomed large. New testimony had just come to light that during the Iran-Contra scandal, that the number three (3) man at the CIA knew what was going on. If true, that put a great big spotlight on Robert Gates. Gates was assistant National Security Adviser under Scrowcroft in the Bush Administration, at the time of his nomination to the CIA. During the Iran-Contra scandal he was the number two (2) man at the CIA as Deputy Director under William Casey. The burning question was how the number one (1) man at the CIA and the number three (3) man had knowledge, but yet the number two (2) man was out of the loop!? Until there were answers provided to the growing list of questions, the hearings were therefore delayed and we were delayed. Parrot said, "If Gates does not get in, there is no way in hell this thing is going forward."

The briefing of agencies continued. Some conducted their own research as to impact and cost. The soundings coming back presented a mixed bag. NASA was now in favor of release. The feeling there was that it would free up money from Congress for future space projects. The Pentagon was firmly against it. The Auditors General's office felt we would be facing $2.5-3 billion in lawsuits from angry citizens and groups feeling they had been lied to and denied access. They anticipated more than 100 lawsuits. We countered that was absurd since the agencies that denied the existence of UFO files did not deliberately deceive; they simply did not know those files existed; besides, those files were properly classified. One could argue 'til hell freezes over whether it should be classified, but not over whether the procedure was proper. It is even quite legal to lie if there is no way to avoid revealing the existence of certain types of classified "black projects." Throughout the month of July 1991, the Gates' hearings kept being delayed, but Bush's support was unwavering. But if the hearings were not going to convene by the end of July, they would have to wait until September because Congress would be in recess during the month of August, which is just what happened. The date was finally set for the 16th of September for the Senate Select Intelligence Committee Hearings on Robert Gates for Director of Central Intelligence (DCI).

As August progressed, feedback from Parrot was that this briefing process was requiring more than anticipated and they would be lucky to finish before Gate's confirmation. They continued to run into obstacles. The Justice Department was against it. The recommendation to Bush would be to take this strictly covertly. Even with the obstacles, the meeting to present the plan was scheduled for the 23rd of August and Raven felt they were ready to approach him. The meeting would take place at Kennebunkport, ME. Bush was there for a working vacation for the month of August. The meeting was to include 15 high level officials from Washington. The hope was that a consensus would swing Bush to "green light" the operation. The meeting was scheduled for 180 minutes; for a perspective an intelligence briefing usually takes 30 minutes or less.

Because of foreign visiting dignitaries, the meeting of the 23rd was delayed. It came down to its third reschedule of the final weekend of the August break. How they could manage to get that many high level officials into Kennebunkport without the press suspecting the advent of WW III, we didn't know. Naturally, the world never sits still while these subjects are being discussed and August was no exception. The Soviet coup attempt and the fall of communism were underway.

My briefing, following the Memorial Day weekend, informed me that the meeting never happened. The news was not good. In essence it was dead, I was told. They shut all the doors and the government locked them. It won't happen at this time. Of the 15 needed to support, they only had four (4). At one time they had eight (8) and thought those eight (8) could convince the other seven (7), but it worked in reverse as they pondered too hard and too long. They made a lot of enemies. When William Webster, the outgoing CIA director, was briefed on the plan he flew into a rage. He kicked a chair and yelled, "You can't do this to me! You can't do this to me! I've had Senators and other high level people sit in that chair and I've told them there is nothing to this! You can't do this to me!" I guess the greater good of an informed public be damned when we had individual reputations to consider. Heron (Jerry Miller) felt Raven hurt himself and that he should have released something first, then watched government circles react. They could not move forward because they had no protection. Bush I, we are told, was never thoroughly briefed. He was only told that a plan was in effect to see if it was feasible to make a release. We were back to plausible deniability.

The reality was that the plan to assess a programmed, gradual release and its projected, potential affects were begun in the 1950s. All the dealings with UFO researchers, planting stories, influencing movie themes, disinformation campaigns, the Emeneggers, Moores and Shanderas had all been the feasibility study. It has been a long-term plan. But, what stops the efforts of Raven and company? It does not seem likely that it is the ETs. It is apparent to us after hours and hours of conversations over many years that the Ebens have a great deal to impart to us. But to make intelligent decisions, the public must be made aware of what is going on. If, as they say, the Ebens are 20-25,000 years advanced beyond us, it is like saying we can not even fathom how far advanced they are. A hundred years ago, we humans could not even envision today's computer age. We cannot predict where we will be in the next 100 years. To even use a number like 25,000 years means their technological, biological and psychological development is incomprehensible to our scientists. But again, by all accounts, the Ebens seem to be helping us. They have given us craft to study and fly. There have been exchange programs. Instead of destroying or conquering, they seem to keep trying to help us.

If that is what the evidence points to then why does each effort for hard evidence get stopped? It does not appear to be the Aviary that is stopping things. It does not appear to be the Ebens that are stopping things; indeed, they seem to go to great lengths to not force us to do anything. But, it does appear as if they are trying to motivate us to perhaps save our planet and ourselves. If they are not here to help us then they are not as smart as their advanced technology would indicate they are. We will find ourselves as short-term playmate without the help of someone else. We are destroying our planet and ourselves; the hard evidence is everywhere, at an exponential rate and incredible speed and on the cosmic scale of time. So, again, what is stopping the evidence from being released? The most logical deduction and conclusion is human greed and power. The old adage goes, "Power corrupts and absolute power corrupts absolutely."

Just think of it, the possibility that ETs could provide new technologies that could not just save but revolutionize the planet. With control of these technologies it could mean world domination. Who better to stop an officially-sanctioned release than power brokers who want continued control? Those who have it are not about to relinquish it.

For our part, we know what exists; we know the reality of the Ebens. Rick Doty has been in intelligence from the inside, he has seen the craft, he has seen the highly classified reports, and he has seen the photos from the

Roswell file showing alien bodies. Bill Moore has seen Unidentified Flying Objects maneuver before him. He has heard incontrovertible testimony from numerous first-hand eye witnesses; he has followed an undeniable trail leading to the inner circle. Jaime Shandera has now had the existence of ETs proven to him beyond question. He has followed much of the same trail as Moore and heard the testimony. But to say that we know beyond what we can prove to the reader is only the first step in a long, long journey. If we are successful with the sources and the investigations with new developments currently underway, the promise of more definitive information will be soon forthcoming.

Jaime Shandera

So what about the forthcoming? Despite the government-Shandera disclosure effort that flopped, what else had taken place since 1991? Starting back in 1987-1988, we were receiving what was called 'Bird Code,' see (5) for samples from the 17+ pages that were received. This Bird Code exchange involved Ernie Kellerstrass, Rick Doty, Robert Collins, Jaime Shandera, Bill Moore and perhaps the DIA's Falcon or the CIA's Walter Ferguson as our Washington DC sources who Bill Moore and Jaime knew, but not the rest of us. This code supposedly gave us directions on how to find the 'Bird Sanctuary' or an apartment in Washington, DC near the mall where an ambassador was kept. Was this ambassador an alien named EBE-3 (female) or some other female EBE who departed in 1989 or was it '93? Needless to say we 'blew' our window of opportunity because some of the information was not interpreted correctly by Jaime Shandera and Bill Moore who actually made the trips to DC.

Jaime started working again on this 'Bird Code' in the early '90s and, with the help of 'postcards' from New Zealand and other places, he was able to put enough information together to make a special trip to Washington in the summer of 1995. It was too late to meet our "ambassador," but it wasn't too late to meet "Mr. X" (Walter Ferguson, CIA?) or was it the DIA's Falcon (supposedly Dale Graff)? Jaime wasn't too clear on that. He met our Mr. X in front of a building near the mall. As Mr. X escorted Jamie into this building, Jaime noticed a checkered board in the front entry way (King's Table) laid in the floor (6) and off to the left was a TS/SCI vault reportedly containing "volumes" on our extraterrestrials. After this trip, he continued to quietly investigate our government's covert involvement with UFOs when in 1999 he finally dropped the whole subject because of mounting pressure to withdraw and the fact that he had just remarried. He has now disavowed himself of the whole UFO subject as far as we know.

References/Footnotes

(1a) The Zeta Reticuli Star System: http://www.ufoconspiracy.com/reports/zetareticuli_star_sys.htm

(b) Colonel John Grine was part of the initial medical team that examined EBE-1. He also assisted in the autopsy on one of the other Ebens. Colonel Grine retired in 1970 and lived in Austin, TX until 1985, when he moved to Albuquerque. Colonel Grine died in 1995 at the age of 91.

(c) Colonel Bryon Redlinger, who lived with EBE-1, died in Phoenix AZ, in 1989. He lived with EBE-1 from 1949 to 1952 when EBE-1 died. Colonel Redlinger was a Captain at the time. Rick said he spoke with him in 1980 and again in 1984. He was a very nice man who retired around 1970. He was from the very old school. He served before WW II. His daughter Dennette lives in Albuquerque and is married to an Air Force officer who must be retired by now. Bill Moore did interview the Colonel sometime back in the 1980-'82 time frame. The agreement was that the interview would be held in confidence and all information would be safeguarded.

(2) As reported in the July 1999 issue of *Physics Today*, two-and-a-half months before his death, the world-renowned Russian physicist Andrei Sakharov gave a speech in Lyons, France. Included in that speech was the following: ".... We are looking into the fantastic possibility that regions of space separated from each other by billions of light years are, at the same time, connected to each other with the help of additional parallel entrances, often called wormholes. In other words, we do not exclude the possibility of a miracle: the instantaneous crossing from one region of space to another. The elapsed time would be so short that we would appear in the new place quite unexpectedly, or, vice versa, someone would suddenly appear next to us. I talk of such things in order to show what kinds of questions are being raised and discussed at the cutting edge of science."

(3) *Project Beta: Creation of a Modern Myth*, Greg Bishop, Paraview Pocket Books 2005.

(4) This is presented for information purposes only: Who is Raven? One strong possibility is that it was Richard Helms (ex-CIA Director) who died in October 2002. Once exposed to the world of UFOs and MJ-12 the word is, "you never retire." Another possible Raven is a scientist who had worked out of Los Alamos for over 30 or was it 50 years?

Why now for all of this? Isn't this just a little outdated? Like so much of the information in this area it's old to some, but new to others, yet in the same breath, this material has never been released before publicly. The narrative in the main text follows the introduction history as a mix of interviews and discussion which was originally done by Jaime Shandera. Jaime's last known place of residence was in San Diego CA living with his present wife, but recently, within the last year or so, he moved back to Los Angeles. Many will complain that "code names" lessen the credibility of the material. This may be true, but the authors have to respect the confidentiality of their sources or else there would be no information. However, in this case, most of the code names have been provided where possible.

(5) Samples of the 'Bird Code' using the exact words. This was the code used by Ernie Kellerstrass, Rick Doty, Bill Moore, a source at DIA and I Robert Collins in an attempt to set up an interview with EBE (female) who was reportedly located in a safe house next to the mall in Washington DC. The Bird Code effort went on from 1987 through 1988. EBE female left in 1989 or '93.

In the beginning there was the Falcon and the Eagle

87/88: In the beginning there were two birds, the Falcon and the Eagle living in the same neighborhood. Their light source shone with two bright nesses. Both birds, although bothered by the Woodpecker, lived happily together in this neighborhood of two bright nesses. At the second phase of their fourth moon trouble began to develop, for the

Eagle became frustrated by the Woodpecker's action. Falcon made its only mistake, for it sided with Woodpecker. A war, which lasted many moon phases, occurred between the Falcon and the Eagle. Once all the feathers were plucked from the Falcon, it became a rare bird. It retired to its nest and slept quietly.

The Eagle Soared

87/88: The Eagle soared above the other birds and made nests in their homes. When the Eagle mated with the Blue Jay, the new breed developed. The new breed and rarest bird is called the Condor. The Condor must open the apartment. For if any other bird opens the door first, the other occupants will flee. The door must be opened with a Special Key mentioned in the third paragraph of the fifth chapter of the written book. The Key will only sleep for one moon phase. Condor must open the door before that time.

The Parrot Spoke Three Times

87/88: The Parrot three times spoke the latter: One in two parts and the Woodpecker taps this message. A few years after tens of thousands of birds flew over Europe: The Eagle acquired three rare birds. Unfortunately one died a few years after. Many years passed while Eagle learned to talk some rare bird: But, mainly the rare bird learned to speak Eagle. These discussions are referred to in the book written in the forth repeat of the twin year the Woodpecker was born.

(6) King's Table game and board : http://www.pbm.com/~lindahl/articles/ kings_table.html

Chapter 5

WILL THE REAL MEN-IN-BLACK (MIB) PLEASE STAND UP?

Ed Doty, the uncle of Rick Doty and a retired AF Colonel who worked for the 7602nd and was involved in the covert collection of UFO reports said, "We learned a lot about the aliens."

The enigmatic "Men-in-Black" is one of the most sinister and controversial areas in UFO research. For many years, stories have surfaced from researchers and from the casual or incidental sightings of UFOs. If UFO pictures were taken, the witnesses sometimes claimed to have been harassed, intimidated and/or the photos were confiscated from them.

Men-in-Black (MIB) are usually reported to travel in groups of three. They are often described as slender, swarthy looking characters of European or Gypsy mien who wore wrap-around sunglasses and drove black Cadillacs or Lincolns which appear out of nowhere only to disappear just as mysteriously. Sometimes they flash government credentials. On other occasions they pose as insurance adjusters, utility company personnel or home repair contractors; plumbers, carpet layers, telephone repairmen, gas line inspectors and even reporters for local newspapers. All are favorite ploys that the MIB were reported to have used. They would invariably appear in an effort to obtain information from people who had a UFO related experience of some sort coming away with physical evidence of the event. This evidence would usually be of a photographic or video nature. The Men-in-Black would often obtain the evidence by means of an empty promise to return it at some future date. If promises failed, they would resort to threats, intimidation, harassment or even surreptitious entry of the home, office or place of business of the witness then they would simply vanish. Some believe they were clandestine government agents, others argue that they are minions of a powerful underground secret society working in tandem with extraterrestrials to take over the planet. A few think they are actually extraterrestrials posing as humans in order to promote some unknown, but invariably sinister agenda.

On the other side are those who claim it is all hogwash; that the whole thing amounts to nothing more than the typical paranoid hysteria invariably associated with the UFO community's lunatic fringe: Most attribute the roots of the legend to the promotion of the late Gray Barker (d, 1984), a sensationalistic UFO folklorist and writer of the '50s and '60s who was well-known for his "spoofs." If anything, it was Barker's book, *They Knew Too Much about Flying Saucers*, (NY: University Books, 1956), plus his numerous pulp magazine articles on the subject which enshrined the Men-in-Black phenomena into the UFO literature. Later, John Keel, a friend of Barker's and a prolific writer of the '60s and '70s who had been known to appear at lecture presentations dressed entirely in black, carried the torch to new heights in his book, *The Mothman Prophecies* (NY: Dutton, 1975).

Curiously, MIB really do exist and they do make occasional appearances to UFO witnesses in order to obtain critical evidence, although such forays are less common than rumor and legend would have us believe. The truth of the matter is that "they" did not create the legend at all, but rather have merely taken opportunistic advantage of it in order to provide cover for their shady operations. As many suspected, they really are government people in disguise. In fact, they were members of a rather bizarre obscure unit of the Air Force Intelligence known in the past as the "Air Force Special Activities Center" (AFSAC). The Air Force Special Activity Center (AFSAC) originated from the Air Force Intelligence Agency, Service, Wing, and Division. Air Force Intelligence started in 1949 after it was the Army Intelligence Group. Various names were changed over the years. AFSAC was devoted primarily to the collection of Human Intelligence or "HUMINT" (i.e., intelligence obtained, often covertly, directly from human sources as opposed to that which has been gathered electronically ELINT). The workings of this unit and its predecessors have long been among the most secretive operations of the military intelligence community. As of 1991, AFSAC, headquartered at Ft. Belvoir ,VA, had been under the operational authority of the Air Force Intelligence Command centered at Kelly Air Force Base in Texas. The obscure history of this unit goes back to at least the early 1950s and perhaps the late 1940s when it was known as the 1006th Air Intelligence Service Squadron. In July 1959, the 1006th became the 1127th Field Activities Group, which in turn became the 7602nd Air Intelligence Group in the early '80s and finally AFSAC around 1983. The Defense Intelligence Agency's (DIA) Defense Humint Services (DHS) eventually absorbed AFSAC in 1999. One or more probable reasons for the periodic reshuffling of names and numbers is to keep the unit's operations as well hidden as possible or it could just be bureaucratic bean counters at work. Many a researcher abandoned the search when an agency or unit appears to have ceased all activity with no indication of its new designation.

There is no question that this group has been connected with the clandestine collection of UFO related information from its earliest inception and that it often made use of three-man teams in its operations (refer back to last chapter on Rick Doty). Indeed, two documents released back in 1991, under the Freedom of Information Act, provide evidence of this. The first of these, AFCIN Policy Letter 205-13 dated 12 April 1960, clearly states that the 1127th "participates in Project Unidentified Flying Object (UFO) in accordance with AFCIN-P1 Policy Letter 205-10, dated 19 January 1960." The second heavily censored FOIA document titled "History of the 1127th Field Activities Group" for 1 January 1960 through 30 June 1960 states on page 20 that, "10 three-man teams (five airborne and five ground) are maintained on an alert roster for the 1127th's Project 'Moon Dust' recovery of space vehicles."

In addition, a curious mid-1960 USAF/OSI (Office of Special Investigation) memorandum on the subject of "Donald E, Keyhoe/Mercury Enterprises, Inc." states unequivocally, "Files relating to UFOs are maintained in two places; at ATIC (Air Technical Intelligence Center) headquarters at Wright-Patterson AFB (Ohio), and at the 1127th Field Activity Group, Ft. Belvoir, VA." AFOSI is an organization whose operations have always been closely allied with those of the 1127th/AFSAC and it is not uncommon for OSI personnel to be assigned to special duty within the unit as they certainly were during the Bennewitz affair.

Even more importantly, according to J.R. Richelson's *The U.S. Intelligence Community* (Cambridge, MA: Ballinger, 1985): "The Air Force Special Activities Center at Ft. Belvoir, Virginia provided centralized management of all Air Force activities involved in the collection of information from human sources. These activities include clandestine collection as well as the debriefing of directors." As mentioned earlier, AFSAC was previously known as the 7602nd Air Intelligence Group and prior to that as the 1127th Field Activities Group. The 1127th was described as "an oddball unit, a composite of special intelligence groups. The men of the 1127th were con artists. Their job was to get people to talk." (The 1127th Field Activities Group had two squadrons: the 1167th and 1116th. The 1167th squadron was headquartered at Weisbaden and contained the following detachments: Det 1, Schierstein; Det 2, Berlin; Det 3, Hahn; Det 4, Wuenheim; Det 5, Oslo and Det 6, Bentwaters. The 1116th squadron was headquartered at Yokota and contained the following detachments: Det 1, Kunsun; Det 2, Saigon; Det 3, Korat Thailand; Det 4, Misawa Japan and Det 4, Laos).

The "oddball unit" description was apt indeed, for con artist they were and still are. Safe crackers, cat burglars, locksmiths, fast talkers, disguise artists, impersonators, assorted masters of deception, eccentric geniuses and useful flakes of all types were recruited from all over the country–even from prison when necessary–in order to staff the unit. Military organizations, discipline and paper work were of secondary importance. The emphasis was always first and foremost the obtaining of information, and those involved were experts at it. They had to be, for they were often assigned to the most dangerous of America's covert intelligence operations.

Since deception was an integral part of their operational strategy, ruses like the Men-in-Black were right up their alley. While it seems unlikely that we shall ever know whose idea it was to adopt the Men-in-Black game for the purpose of obtaining UFO information, it was almost certainly Gray Barker's early '50s hype that inspired it. All the 1127th had to do was adopt the concept and use it for their purposes. The sensationalistic paranoia of the UFO community and the accompanying incredulity of more responsible individuals would provide all the cover they needed. No one but the lunatic fringe would ever believe such stories were true and the 1127th knew that the fringe groups had little credibility outside their own small circles. It was the perfect cover. Again, this fitted the operational mandate to control the evidence.

During late 1979-1983, the 1127th successor unit, the 7602nd Air Intelligence Group, was heavily involved in the Paul Bennewitz affair as mentioned previously, but so were AFOSI and several other agencies, most notably the National Security Agency (NSA). Also, Charles Doty and Ed Doty, father and uncle of Rick Doty both retired AF Colonels worked for the 7602nd and were heavily involved in the covert collection of UFO reports.

Since AFSAC was merged under the Defense Intelligence Agency's (DIAs) Defense Humint Services (DHS, subdivided into three regional areas within the US) in 1999, can we assume that part of its job is to collect UFO reports covertly. For further reading see references.

Mythology or otherwise, the MIB have played a significant role in the world of Flying Saucer folklore wearing many different faces, human and otherwise, and representing a part of the so often talked about "Shadow Government."

So, what better a shadow than things which lie beneath, a macabre mystery which is all their own? We will see how true this might be in Section 3.

References/Footnotes

Nick Redfern: *On the Trail of the Saucer Spies: Ufos And Government Surveillance*, Anomalist Books (February 28, 2006).

SECTION III: WHAT LIES BENEATH?

Chapter 1

THE VAULTS AT WRIGHT-PATTERSON AFB

The military presence began there in 1917 when Wilbur Wright Field was opened on the site of today's flight line to train pilots, armories, and gunners during World War I. A depot also began operating there. Aviation research and development continued to flourish there as well. First, McCook Field was built at what is now the intersection of State Route 4 and Interstate 75. Then Wilbur Wright Field was established where the present runway is in 1924, on land donated by the local community. Wilbur Wright Field and the depot area became Patterson Field on July 6, 1931, in honor of Lt. Frank Patterson. He was killed in 1918 in the flight line crash of a DH-4 while flight-testing the synchronization of machine gun and propeller. In 1948, Wright and Patterson fields were merged and created to form Wright-Patterson AFB.

Today, as in the early 1900s, Wright-Patterson is where weapon systems of the future are conceived, tested and modified by the base's 10,000 researchers, scientists, and engineers. Wright-Patterson has evolved into the largest, most diverse and organizationally complex base in the Air Force. The Air Force missions range from logistics management, research and development, education, flight operations, and many other defense related activities. Wright-Patterson AFB is the home of the headquarters of a vast worldwide logistics system supporting the entire Air Force. It also has the foremost aeronautical research and development center in the Air Force.

Wright-Patterson AFB has a work force numbering approximately 24,000 people, making it the fifth largest employer in the state of Ohio and the largest employer at a single location. It is home for more than 70 units representing seven (7) different Air Force commands and a host of DOD organizations. The base pays out nearly $3 million in salaries every day of the year totaling an annual payroll of approximately $1.2 billion (1). This brief history alone tells the reader that not only is Wright-Patterson of central importance today, but it had equal, if not greater importance in July 1947. In 1947, most of the Air Force research and development (R & D) took place "in-house" meaning only those in military uniform performed the basic R and D for aircraft and rocket-missile development. This method guaranteed the utmost secrecy for any programs deemed sensitive.

On July 8, 1947, Col. Blanchard announced a flying saucer had been captured near Roswell, NM, on that late afternoon; J. Bond Johnson took General Ramey's photograph in Fort Worth with a copy of the message apparently just sent to Hoyt Vandenberg in his hand. While Ramey told the world that a weather balloon went down in Roswell, the Army general had in his hand a memo telling Pentagon brass of a "disc" crash with "victims."

After the reported Roswell recovery of aliens and their flying saucer in July of 1947, the many stories and rumors suggested that these artifacts were brought to WPAFB in Dayton, OH. Recent information seems to add substantial credence to those reported rumors in the form of a message virtually pulled from General Ramey's hand by means of digital enhancement (thanks to David Rudiak) (2). The message to Vandenberg reads, see next page:

17:13 CST   ARMY CABLE
A) URGENT
B) HQAAF
C) WASHINGTON
D) 8 JUL 1947
E) VANDENBERG
F) FROM: HQ 8TH AAF
G) SUB: ROSWELL

0) FWAAF ACKNOWLEDGES THAT A "DISK" IS NEXT NEW FIND WEST OF
1) THE CORDON. AT LOCATION WAS A WRECK NEAR OPERATION AT THE
2) "RANCH" AND THE VICTIMS OF THE WRECK YOU FORWARDED TO THE
3) ??TEAM AT FORT WORTH, TEX.

4) AVIATORS IN THE "DISC" THEY WILL SHIP FOR A1/8TH ARMYAMHC
5) BY B29-ST OR C47. WRIGHT AF ASSESS AIRFOIL AT ROSWELL. ASSURE
6) THAT CIC/TEAM SAID THIS MISSTATE MEANING OF STORY AND THINK
7) LATE TODAY NEXT SENT OUT PR OF WEATHER BALLOONS WOULD FARE
8) BETTER IF THEY ADD LAND DEMORAWIN CREWS.
9) RAMEY

TOP SECRET

To add credence that something of tremendous importance was occurring in July 1947, we have from Edward Ruppelt's book *The Report on Unidentified Flying Objects*, 1956 the following: "By the end of July 1947, the UFO security lid was down tight. The few members of the press who did inquire about what the Air Force was doing got the same treatment that you would get today if you inquired about the number of thermonuclear weapons stock-piled in the U.S.'s atomic arsenal. No one, outside of a few high-ranking officers in the Pentagon, knew what the people in the barbed wire enclosed Quonset huts that housed the Air Technical Intelligence Center (this should of read T2 Intelligence in Ruppelt's book) were thinking or doing," (Chapter 2, page 22). Furthermore, two other sources support the fact that wreckage and bodies were brought to WP. They are, a MAJIC (Military Assessment of the Joint Intelligence Committee) memo dated 19 SEP 1947 and the June Crain story, http://209.132.68.98/pdf/crain_clarksoninterview.pdf.

If the Roswell material were brought to Wright-Patterson AFB, the next logical question would be: stored where? The folklore rumors state that it was "Hangar 18." Through many years of intensive effort, the only evidence we found to support such stories were a series of buildings called 18 A, B, C, etc., but no Hangar 18. However, other evidence supports the idea that buildings 18 A, B, C, etc. may have had something to do with our "Little Green Men" as the stories go, but it wasn't Hangar 18. Instead, it was called Hangar 23: Hangar 23 sits between buildings 18F and 18A in the 18 Complex. The story goes that the Roswell or other alien craft(s) (dimensions of ~ 30 x 15 ft disc) were brought into Hangar 23. The floor of the hangar was removed and the craft(s) were lowered into this newly dug-out basement. A concrete floor was then placed over this basement area containing the craft(s). At the same time, an entry way was built from a vault in the east basement of building 18A to this new basement in Hangar 23. All the above was said to have been done in record time. According to the drawings, there is a basement in this building, but it is small compared to the size needed for these reported alien craft(s). But, this was expected in an unclassified drawing.

Hangars normally don't have basements, but this hangar was converted into an office building (it's now the AF Research Laboratory, Sensor Directorate, Target Signature Branch), then back in the late '70s or early '80s it appears that a smaller basement was installed in a much larger basement. Also, the drawings of the east basement of 18F do show a vaulted door in that exact same area. If Hangar 23 is not the only place where "UFO artifacts" might have been brought to, then where else?

On a 1954 Area B map of WPAFB not shown (note: the WP Civil Engineering person lost his security clearance by supplying offical drawings to this author) one can see Hangar 4 or Hangars 4A, B and C (see Figure 2). Hangar 4 was reported to be just a holding area until they could move the recovered "artifacts" to their final destination. Where might that have been?

Figure 2: Hangars 4A, B and C

With the help of some very reliable sources–including Rick Doty and Ernie Kellerstrass and a number of other people, plus technical support in the form of drawings–we believe that we may have found underground vaults in Area B of WPAFB. After thousands of hours and years of extensive investigations, we found this underground vault system to be quite extensive and very well maintained due to substantial "black funds." This was true up until circa 1982/83 when evidence suggests the remaining artifacts were removed and the vaults permanently sealed. On a historical note, these vaults were already reportedly present at the time of the Roswell incident and were used to store nitrate film. Considering its potentially explosive nature, what better place than 40 feet below ground under limestone rock where it is naturally cool.

Limestone, sedimentary rock wholly or in large part composed of calcium carbonate. It is ordinarily white but may be colored by impurities such as iron oxide making it brown, yellow, or red and carbon making it blue, black, or gray. The texture varies from coarse to fine. Most limestone is formed by the deposition of sedimentary rock, wholly or in large part composed of calcium carbonate.

At this point it's important for the readers to understand that even when one has access to certain facilities and drawings it doesn't automatically mean one can just walk in and start "busting down" walls to prove one's point. Wright-Patterson AFB is still U.S. government property.

Those Nitrate Film Vaults

Besides the two above ground **Nitrate Film** storage vaults at WP (Located in Area "B") (now used for keeping exposed nitrate film safe from deterioration until their contents can be transferred to a "safe film"), there were a number of other nitrate film storage vaults below ground that were reportedly built in the mid-'30s designed for massive storage of nitrate film. For nitrate film please see, http://ufoconspiracy.com/ reports/nitrate_film.pdf. It was in 1947, and later, that these film storage vaults (later converted) were reportedly used to store the recovered "alien bodies" from Roswell and other crash sites. These underground storage vaults were only known for the most part by a few people in the photographic detachment at the time (reference conversations with one of the "vault curators" who is now long retired and probably deceased).

Now, directing the reader's attention to Figure 3, this modified WP drawing is based on source data and overhead imagery. We will use this drawing for our guided tour of these Area B underground vaults.

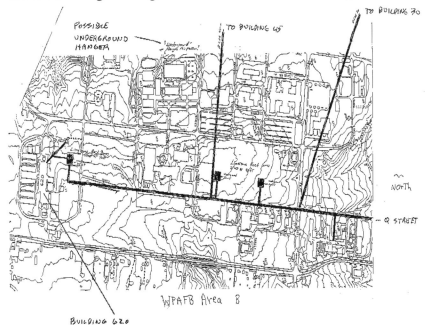

Figure 3: Wright-Patterson AFB Drawing Modified

Avionics Building 620

By starting first with Bldg 620 (Avionics Bldg), on the south end of Area B we will work our way approximately north, then west, and then north again along this tunnel system connecting this reported underground vault system.

One entrance to this underground vault system, according to sources who have worked or been in building 620, was down a set of stairs under the avionics tower. These stairs were blocked as of 1982. There were two freight-sized elevators under the avionics tower. One went to go a second basement area. This "other" freight elevator was reportedly removed in the mid to late '70s. Ernie Kellerstrass (Ret USAF Lt Col) said he was down in this area during the 1972-74 time frames. There were key inserts in this elevator with one used solely for second basement access. Ernie mentioned that he used the stairs and not the elevator at that particular moment.

In Figure 4, we have a detailed drawing of what is the north first floor entry of Bldg 620 to this underground vault system then through a second basement area. The depiction shows entry from a classified first basement which is actually a second basement. Also, the rectangle marked, "Very Large Vaulted Room" should read "40 ft" not, "20 ft beneath parking lot" with a "g" missing from "parking."

Figure 5 shows a picture of this north entry on the west side of the building under the avionics tower with the West Auditorium off to the right. The reader will note the new construction taking place in 1998. Those walls go down about 30 feet, but this new basement area avoids the area where the tunnel and vault would be approximately 40 feet down. There is a parking lot over this vault. See Figure 6 for location of parking lot and vault.

Figure 4: Underground Vault near building 620.

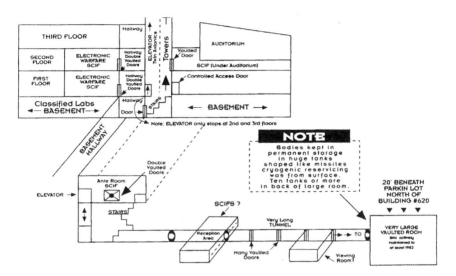

This is a diagram of how the underground vaults at Wright-Patterson AFB are constructed. Originally used for highly flammable nitrate film. They were ideal for conversion to alien cold storage.

Figure 5: Building 620 expansion; northwest corner 1998.

Figure 6: Parking lot over laid over vault near building 620

The construction team at the time was complaining about the walls rolling which affected the new construction, and the reason given was the poor foundation filler. But privately, these same contractors were saying they suspected underground structures. Perhaps one more reason for the walls rolling in this case surfaced when an unknown drawing or site plan was found for the years 1972/73 as an addition to Bldg 620. This plan was not a proposal, according to Wright-Patterson Civil Engineers (CE), because it was common practice not to keep proposals on file. This addition sits exactly where the new addition to Bldg 620 sits today. We don't know if this 72/73 addition is well below ground or if, in fact, it exists at all. But then, there is a drawing for it. Perhaps the answer may lie in someone's vault?

Double Vaulted Doors and a Tunnel?

Ernie reported that a set of double vaulted doors led to a long hallway with a second set of double vaulted doors to an anteroom elevator and stairs, and then a long tunnel that led to one of the main vaults under the north parking lot of Bldg 620 (Figures 4, 7 and 8). In the Figure 7 and 8 drawings there is an unidentified extension in silhouette going away from the building on the north side just under the avionics tower. WPAFB CE sources stated that they had no idea what this extension meant, but this "silhouette" is in the shape of a hallway going in the direction of the reported tunnels/vaults. This extension away from the building also showed up on NASA imagery that was taken at the request of Wright Labs to test a new Synthetic Aperture Ground Penetrating Radar System (see section on Ground Penetrating Radar on page 136).

Before Bldg 620 was built in the early '60s, the primary reported entry at this end was through an old wooden building called 618 which was torn down after 620 was built. Bldg 618 appears on a 1954 Area B map and was directly in line with the reported north-south tunnel with Bldg 618 on a straight line from Hangar 4. There has since been a new Bldg 618 built which is attached to the east side of Bldg 620. This new 618 is not lined up with the reported north-south tunnel.

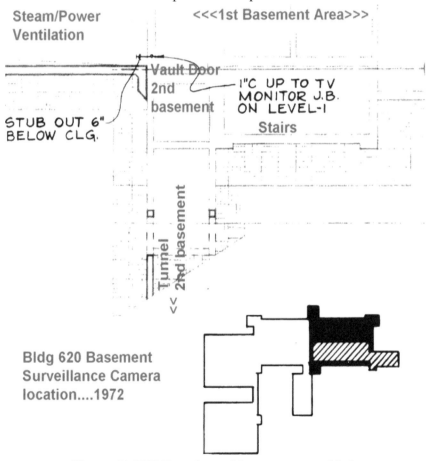

Figure 7: WP Drawing with comments added.

124

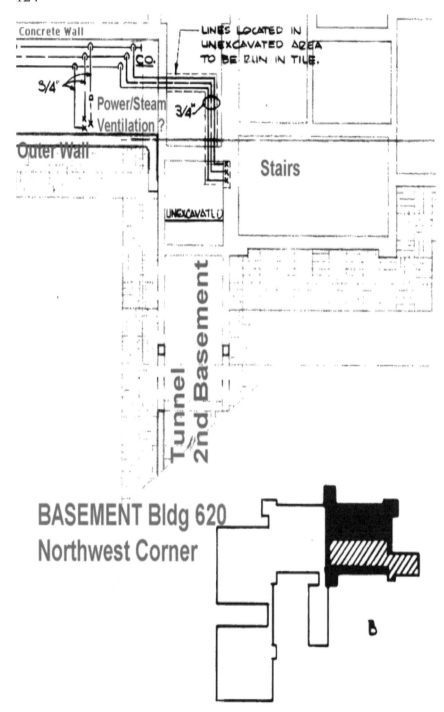

Figure 8: WP Drawing with comments added.

Backup Entry for Closed-Up Vault Near Building 620

A WPAFB Civil Engineering (CE) source attempted to gain access to this blocked area in December 1992 by going through the first basement to an East Basement Vaulted Lab area. By going through this East Basement Lab, they reached the area they were looking for, but it was blocked by 2-inch steel bars placed there for security reasons according to the security manager in Bldg 620. The steel bars blocked a tunnel leading approximately west-northwest back to where the double vaulted doors would have been in the reported second basement area (Figure 9). However, on a second trip, that blocked area with the steel bars had since been walled up (see Figure 10).

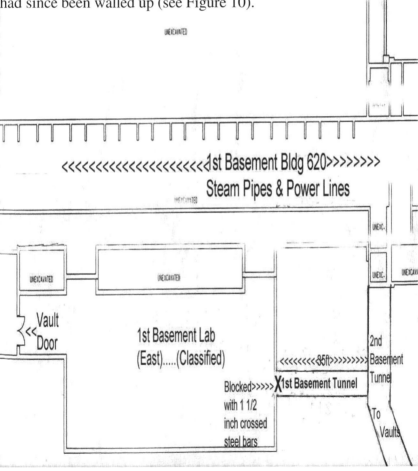

Figure 9: WP Drawing with comments added.

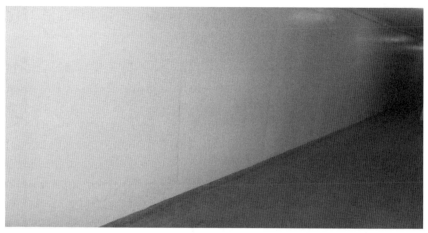

Figure 10: First basement west vault showing newly walled up area.

Moving away from building 620, we go next to building 45. This building was once the Wright Laboratory Headquarters in 1982. Currently it is the Air Force Research Laboratory's (AFRL) Air Vehicles Directorate, Integration and Operations Division, Technology Integration Branch.

Here we will deviate from the previous way of reporting things and instead let Rick Doty, who worked in Air Force Counter-Intelligence and now a retired MSgt, give us a description of a visit he made to WPAFB on a rainy day in May 1982.

Figure 11: Back of Bldg 45: Vault is located under this parking lot.

"We had lunch at the WPAFB Officer's Club. We then drove over to the Foreign Technology Division (FTD) now the National Air and Space Intelligence Center (NASIC) to pick-up an AF Lt. Colonel at Detachment 22. The Lt. Colonel escorted the others and myself over to a huge red brick building (Bldg 45) in Area B of WPAFB. This building was about a half mile from the fire truck wash rack. We parked by some trees in the front of the building. We went up a set of brick stairs and through a pair of heavy doors with glass windows (front entry of Bldg 45). We then went down a set of stairs into the basement and then through a set of hallways (see arrowed pathway in Figure 12).

Bldg. 45, Wright-Patterson AFB, OH; Basement Area

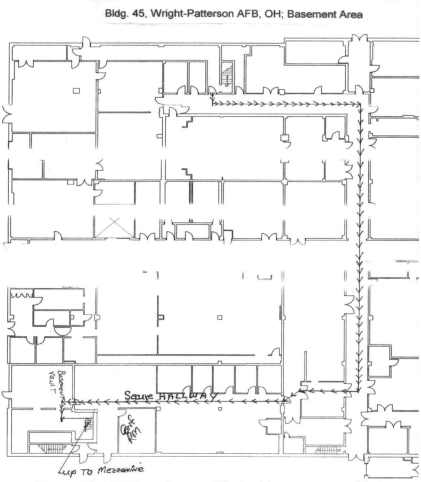

Figure 12: WP Drawing modified with comments added.

"We finally arrived at the 'secure hallway' where the first badge check was done. We then went past a small auditorium and into a small vaulted room and then up another set of stairs into another vaulted room (mezzanine) and then down again using the stairs even though there was an elevator available. At the bottom, we went through another check point before going through a very long tunnel about 90 to 120 feet with multiple bank-sized vault doors. This tunnel system had carpeting all along its length and wide enough to drive a pick-up truck through. We then entered an anteroom where we were checked again. There were a lot of people working in this area (Bob Fugate accompanied me on this trip). We then proceeded down the remaining tunnel, which forked at a guard duty station. We forked to the left down another tunnel into a huge vaulted room estimated to be 100 x 100 feet at least. In this huge vault room, I estimated there to be at least 20 vats, and I couldn't be sure all the vats were in use. This huge room had vertical tanks that looked like missiles on the opposite side of the room. On the right, as you entered this huge room, were four to five horizontal tubes that looked like lung breathers. The vertical "missile tubes" were surrounded by what looked like cryogenic liquid, i.e., liquid nitrogen? The vertical tubes extended to the ceiling approximately 10 feet high. They opened up a few of the "lung breathers" or caskets. In the first one, the alien body was so badly cut-up from all the autopsy work that I got sick to my stomach. In the second casket, the body was in much better shape and looked exactly like what was shown in the "FTD alien graphics (refer back to Section 2 Chapter 4). Those graphics reportedly originated from the Foreign Technology Division at Wright-Patterson Air Force Base."

This vault was very similar to the one located at Ft. Belvoir "Annex K" which is in a remote area of Washington, DC, or Virginia. Rick mentioned that he had been to so many of these facilities that he would get the particulars mixed-up. It seems the Air Force builds underground SCI facilities like they build chow halls.

In connection with Ft Belvoir, we reference a Wilber Smith (Canadian "Project Magnet") and we quote, "According to Smith's son Jim Smith, shortly before his death in 1962, Wilbert called his son in and told him that he had in fact seen the alien bodies from a crash, and had been shown a crashed flying saucer outside of Washington D.C." See, "Wilber Smith Interview and Draft of Wilbert Smith Top Secret UFO Memo" now public at, http://www.presidentialufo.com/top_secret_draft.htm.

Medical Doctor Paid Hush Money by DOJ?

It has also been reported that most, if not all, of the MDs who did the alien autopsy work are being paid hush money by the Justice Department out of "black funds." An MD by the name of Robert T. Crowley is one example of this. Dr. Crowley was born in 1910 and is more than likely deceased. We have a personal transcript of Bill Moore's interview with Crowley back in December 1981 in which Crowley openly admitted to getting a check from the Justice Department.

Buildings 450, 29 & 30

Moving north, we come to Bldg 450 the Flight Dynamics Lab (reference Figure 13). Not much is known about this building other than it does have a second basement. There is another reported tunnel going off in the direction of Bldg 30 close to Medical Bldg 29 (refer back to Figure 3). Near buildings 29 and 30 is a reported small vault that allegedly was used for VIP viewing going all the way back to the Eisenhower era.

Figure 13: Building 450

"Mandible" maybe Alien: Was it from WP?

See letter below signed by technician, Bruce Phillips, for his interpretation of photos, comparing alien and human mandibles.

Sketches of Mandible
—— By John Mosgrove

Figure 1: Top view of mandible. Portion below dotted line was molded into a study model. Above dotted line is missing portion of a widening jawbone.

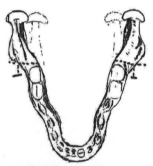

Figure 2: Bottom view of mandible's arch. Dotted line separates missing and the duplicated sections.

B. P. DENTAL LABORATORY

CASE STUDY OF THE TWO MODELS.
IN PICTURE, Model MOUNTED ON ARTICULATOR is WHITE MALE APPROX. 30 YEARS OLD. AVERAGE SIZED ADULT MALE. BOTH MODELS ARE LOWER MANDibular ARCHES.

(ADULT MALE)
DIFFERENCES
A) TEETH: INCISORS for CUTTING MEAT ECT.
B) ARCH SHAPE U HORSE SHOE SHAPE
C) ARCH DEPTH LESS DEEP.

(UNKNOWN)
DIFFERENCES
A) TEETH; FLAT PLANE, NO CUTTING SURFACES
B) ARCH SHAPE U RADICAL SHAPED ARCH
C) ARCH DEPTH, MUCH DEEPER

PERSONAL OPINION
I'VE WORKED IN THE DENTAL FIELD FOR OVER 20 YEARS, AND I'VE NEVER RUN ACROSS ANYTHING ANIMAL OR HUMAN THAT COMPARE TO THE MODEL IN QUESTION.

BRUCE A. Phillips C.D.T, B.S.

Figure 14: Unknown and human mandible compared

Dental Technician says "Mandible" maybe Alien

John K. Mosgrove is a 67 year-old dental technician currently living in Richmond, Indiana as of 1994. In 1979, he says, while working at a Veterans Administration hospital in Dayton, Ohio (about a 30 minute drive from Wright Patterson Air Force Base), he was assigned the task of replicating a strange mandible, or lower jawbone, taken from a creature of unknown identity. Under orders to remain silent, he told no one about these events for over 14 years; but he did create additional copies of the strange mandible for future study. Carl Day of Dayton's WDTN Channel 2 ran two special reports on Mosgrove in 1994 and has continued to investigate the possible legitimacy of the "alien" mandible.

After Mosgrove had made the replica and gave it to the doctor he peered out the little window in the door. He saw a Major and Lt Col in full military uniform. The doctor handed the replica to them, shook hands with them, and they left. Mosgrove said he'd seen the Lt. Colonel before, trying to decide where it was. It was either at the VA Hospital or it was at Wright-Pat.

Mosgrove could tell from the original impression that this person, or whatever it was, was in a terrible accident, or got hit, because of the bone fragments. "This thing had a terrible hit in the face, like slamming into something. The main part of the force that hit the face would have been more to the upper than the lower. This knocked the teeth out, but it didn't break the mandible. So that means an indirect hit. If there was anything broken on this lower arch, it would have been the hinge and not particularly the jaw bone."

He said the teeth that were left in the mandible were all flat-planed, which would mean that there was no reason for incisors to tear. Just a kind of grinding was all they would need, which would mean that they were plant eaters. "The most striking part of the thing was the shape of the mandible. If you would put tissue on this — you know how you see on TV when people have drawn aliens and they all have little, real pointed chins — that's exactly how it would look.

You would have a pointed, very small chin area, and wider where it connected to the temporal mandibular arch."

I've never seen an alien. But due to the shape and the contour of this thing, and considering where it came from, I don't know what else it could be. It's not animal, and I know it's not human. It's not a freak. This mandible has been around for awhile, because you could see the pit holes in the bone from being dried out. I think it's been around for at least 50 years (editor: from the Roswell crash?).

Nothing I've ever seen looks like this mandible Mosgrove said. "Can I say it's alien? No. But I have to say there is something hush-hush about this mandible. Putting two and two together, that makes one very suspicious."

For a higher resolution picture of this mandible see, http://www.ufoconspiracy.com/images/mandiblealien.jpg

Flying Saucer Wind Tunnel Testing at Wright-Patterson AFB in 1947

In the Figure 15 document (p. 134) is page 1 of 2 (second page is not shown) and comes from an 80-page package containing declassified documents with declassified dates ranging from 1950-'94. Some of the declassified documents detail Counter Intelligence Corps (CIC) collection requirements or information gathered on the **Horten Brother's Flying Wing type aircraft**. The document makes reference to what are called EEI or "Essential Elements of Information" which gives a background of "what to look for" in gathering information or "what has been found" on "flying wing type aircraft" which includes "flying saucers." Although these reports mix the subject of flying wings and saucers together there was never any evidence that the Germans tested "flying saucer" type aircraft. We quote from a declassified Army document (not shown) marked "**SECRET:** HEADQUARTERS BERLIN COMMAND, OFFICE OF MILITARY GOVERNMENT FOR GERMANY (US) BERLIN, GERMANY, S-2 Branch, **APO 742, US ARMY** dated 16 December 47 with the subject: Horton Brothers (Flying Saucers). Sent to: Deputy Director of Intelligence European Command, Frankfurt APO 757, US Army)."

The document said: "As far as the flying saucer is concerned, a number of people were contacted in order to verify whether or not any such design at any time was contemplated or existed in the files of any German air research institute. The people contacted included the following: Walter Horten; Fraulien von der Groeben, former Secretary to Air Force; General Udet Guenter Heinrich, former office for research of the High Command of the Air Force in Berlin; Professor Betz, former chief of Aerodynamic Institute in Goettingen Eugen, former test pilot.

"All the above mentioned people contacted independently and at different times are very insistent on the fact that to their knowledge and belief no such design ever existed nor was projected by any of the German air research institutions. While they agree that such a design would be highly practical and desirable, they do not know anything about its possible realization now or in the past."

However, the "flying saucer" wind tunnel testing reference document (Figure 15 again) seems to have originated from a belief that "flying saucers" were real and fits with what another independent source reported or, Ernie Kellerstrass. Ernie said that in 1953 and 1954, while at WP, he saw "wind tunnel UFO models" of all different shapes and sizes laid out on a table ready for testing: These "wind tunnel models" were said to be of "flying wings," "deltoids," etc., as well as the typical "flying saucers." The wind tunnel test facility was located in Area "A" and later in Area "B," see, Figure 16.

UNCLASSIFIED

CONFIDENTIAL

HEADQUARTERS
970TH COUNTER INTELLIGENCE CORPS DETACHMENT
EUROPEAN COMMAND

File: D-198239

APO 757
28 October 1947

SUBJECT: FLYING SAUCERS

TO : See Distribution

1. Inclosed EEI written at WRIGHT FIELD, Ohio, concerning flying saucers, is forwarded for compliance therewith. The Air Materiel Command is of the opinion that some sort of object, such as the flying saucer, did exist. At the present time, construction models are being built for wind tunnel tests.

2. Attention is directed to unnumbered paragraphs 4 and 5 of the referenced EEI.

a. The HORTEN Brothers, Walter and Reimar (Possibly Rainer), are believed to be in the British Zone. However, one HORTEN Ing (Probably Walter) has been reported to be living at LANDSHUT, Germany.

b. EEI lists HEILEGENBERG and GOTHA, Germany as places where experiments were conducted by the Germans, concerning planes designed by the HORTEN Brothers. Records, this headquarters, indicate that activities were also conducted at GOTTINGEN, Germany; that several planes were built, and that other testing grounds for the HORTEN planes were LEIPZIG BRANDIS, HERSFELD BEBRA, HORNBERG (Black Forest) and ÆGIDIENBERG/BONN. All these places are located in Germany outside the U. S. Zone.

c. A Lieutenant SCHEIDTHAUER, formerly of the German Forces, is known to have been the test pilot of some of the planes.

3. It is suggested that all of your files concerning developments of aircraft by the Soviets be reviewed for possible leads.

Regraded CONFIDENTIAL by authority of
(Col.) Clay III by Bli
on 1-31-51
L.E. Phillips 2d Lt ORDC

BEST COPY AVAILABLE

REGRADED UNCLASSIFIED
ON 6F IIII 1994
BY CDR USAINSCOM F01/PO

CONFIDENTIAL

Figure 15

Figure 16: Air Force historical photo.
Former Wright Air Development Division systems engineers make some final adjustments on the 20-inch hypersonic wind tunnel in Bldg. 450, Area B before they test the aerodynamics of a futuristic aircraft design on Oct. 13, 1960.

The Avrocar and other Aerodynes

Figure 17: Avrocar Photo.
The Avrocar photo in Figure 17 was not taken at Wright Field; it shows the vehicle ready for testing in the 40 x 80 feet Ames Labs (Cleveland, OH) subsonic wind tunnel. According to the rumors and hearsay, the Figure 17 photo supposedly showed, "irrefutable proof that the United States had captured extraterrestrial spaceships and stored them in the mythological Hangar 18." During the Avrocar-Silverbug fiasco, engineers soon learned that there were major difficulties understanding how a saucer shaped craft could move within our atmosphere. So, whether flying saucers exist or not, they

certainly cannot use the same propulsion or lifting technology as either our jet aircraft or rockets.

After 50 years, all we have are Harrier, Sukhoi, other VTOL aircraft, UAVs and some circular drones with a central propeller, which are being flown and undoubtedly mistaken for extraterrestrial spacecraft on occasion, but no functional supersonic flying saucer of terrestrial origin except for those being flight tested at Area 51-S4 (3).

Structures and Ground Penetrating Radar

In September of 1995, an aircraft over flew Area B of WPAFB equipped with Synthetic Aperture Radar or Long Wavelength Ground Penetrating Synthetic Aperture Radar. Wright-Patterson civil engineering commented that the image from this scan turned-up a large number of underground structures in Area B. The first image overlay showed tunnel structures near both Bldg 620 and Bldg 450. The underground shots only went down 20 to 30 feet. The second scan went down 50 to 100 feet in April of 1996. Those image scans come in two versions: sanitized and un-sanitized. The U.S. Air Force will say there is only one version.

Ground penetrating radar (GPR, sometimes called ground probing radar, georadar, subsurface radar or Earth sounding radar) is a noninvasive, electromagnetic geophysical technique for subsurface exploration, characterization and monitoring history. It is widely used in locating lost utilities, environmental site characterization and monitoring, agriculture, archaeological and forensic investigation, unexploded ordnance and land mine detection, groundwater, pavement and infrastructure characterization, mining, ice sounding, permafrost, void, cave and tunnel detection, sinkholes, subsidence and a host of other applications. It may be deployed from the surface by hand or vehicle, in boreholes, between boreholes, from aircraft and from satellites. It has the highest resolution of any geophysical method for imaging the subsurface, with even centimeter scale resolution sometimes possible (4).

Open areas in Area "B" of Wright-Patterson AFB

Figure 18: Area B
See locations marked with an "X" where nothing has ever been built over the years except parking lots and tennis courts and at one time they had old wooden-type WWII barracks in some of these areas. Space for expansion in this part of Area "B" is a precious commodity

and what really sticks out like a "sore thumb" is the area marked with the middle "X": This is a huge open field. From all the initial research and reports there are two good-sized vaults 40ft down under a limestone rock dome and another vault located where the top "X" is next to building 620 as discussed previously. Notice how all three "Xs" line up.

As we mentioned in the beginning, one cannot simply break down walls in a government facility. In the case of these reported vaults, although reportedly sealed, the mere existence of them is a threat to the security of the subject. On October 13, 1994, a pair of AFOSI agents walked into the CE office at WPAFB and presented the CE person there with a complete transcript of our phone conversations for the last several days.

Dr. Eric Wang

Very little is known about Dr. Eric Wang, but he was an Austrian-born graduate of the Vienna Technical Institute, and a close associate of Victor Schauberger who had developed a concept of a flying disc and worked on the supposed German flying disc program (lots of doubt about this program) as early as 1941. Wang taught structural and metallurgical engineering at the University of Cincinnati from 1943 to 1952. Dr. Wang supposedly examined some of the recovered crashed discs and compared them to the vehicles tested in the German V-7 program, but found the retrieved craft to be different in nature. In 1949, he became director of the Department of Special Studies at Wright-Patterson where he worked long hours in cooperation with scientists from the "Office of Naval Research" and with Dr. Vannevar Bush and others from the "Research and Development Board." Dr. Wang relocated his research from Wright-Patterson to Kirtland AFB in Albuquerque, NM. He passed away on December 4, 1960.

Area 51 at WP Army Air Force Base in 1945

Reference the Figure 19 drawing/map showing Area 51 at Wright-Patterson: This was extracted from a January 1945 Wright Field Project Sanitary Sewerage Investigation and Report, Master Sanitary Sewerage Plan: Done by the, "U.S. Engineering Office, Cincinnati Ohio: File

No. O-P 1175-1/2." This Area 51 is known to be on maps prior to 1945 and on maps up to at least 1948. This WP Area 51 was located in what is known today as "Area B." The drawing runs almost directly east/west and sits on a hill which over looks the Wright Field flight line as it was in 1945. WP Area 51 is right next to an "acceleration runway/ramp" which was used for rocket sled testing. That ramp is still present today but isn't used. Also, Area 51 sits right next to a reported underground hangar(s) built during WW II so that aircraft could be moved underground in case of an enemy air attack. Before and after 1945 Wright-Patterson AFB was known as a major military R & D center and many German scientist, and engineers under "Project PAPERCLIP" were brought there after WW II to work on various classified projects.

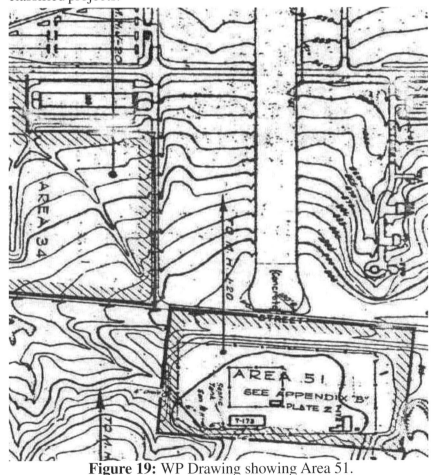

Figure 19: WP Drawing showing Area 51.

Other programs/projects that could have been supported at WP, before the reported Roswell recovery of July 1947, were the IPU or the "Interplanetary Phenomenon Unit" headquartered out of Ft. Carson, CO (5).

Can we draw any conclusions? The illustrations speak for themselves, so the reader is left with their own personal interpretations for what it might all mean. Can it be said that Wright-Patterson is one of the few places that attest to the fact that in July 1947, UFO artifacts were brought there for the sole purpose of scientific research and exploitation? Speculation is that the government packed up all of its alien artifacts in the 1982-83 time frame and moved them elsewhere like Los Alamos and/or Area 51. Was Wright-Patterson AFB the only place where things alien were kept? Both Los Alamos and Area 51 are said to play equally important parts as we shall see in the next Chapters (6), (7).

References/Footnotes

1) For more on Wright-Patterson AFB see the following links: http://www.globalsecurity.org/military/facility/wright-pat.htm, http://www.strategic-air-command.com/bases/Wright-Patterson_AFB.htm and http://www.ascho.wpafb.af.mil/buildings/buildings.htm

2) Roswell Proof: http://roswellproof.homestead.com/

3a) "Project Silverbug:" http://www.laesieworks.com/ifo/lib/AVRO-Silverbug.html

b) "Project SILVERBUG" report: Joint Wright Air Development Center – Air Technical Intelligence Center Report on Project Silver Bug, Technical Report No. TR-AC-47, project No. 9961, dated 15-Feb-1955. Presents technical data on A. V. Roe, Canada, Limited, design proposal for development Project Y2, a circular platform, flat-riser aircraft.

4) *GRORADAR: Processing, Modeling and Display of Dispersive Ground Penetrating Radar Data.* Copyright© 1997-2002 by Gary R. Olhoeft.

5) Counter Intelligence Corps/Interplanetary Phenomenon Unit Report at: http://209.132.68.98/pdf/ipu_report.pdf 22 July 1947 (415k). This seven-page document by the Interplanetary Phenomenon Unit begins by saying "….,the extraordinary recovery of fallen airborne objects in the State of New Mexico between 4 July and 6 July 1947."

6) As a further concluding remark for this chapter, both Tim Cooper's father MSgt Harry B. Cooper, now deceased, and Jim Angleton's grandfather (James Jesus Angleton, Section 2, Chapter 1), also deceased in 1987, have both described early government work involving teleportation experiments. One such set of experiments was said to have taken place at Wright-Patterson AFB in the early '60s. Needless to say, those early experiments ended up in disaster where solid innate matter was turned inside out as did the animals they used in the experiments. Jim Angleton's grandfather JJA, who is mentioned above, related the following with Jim reading from his CIA notes: "The first transport blew up a rat. It literally blew up into pieces. A visitor (Alien) helped them tweak the dimensions to send the rat from point 'a' to point 'b.' But as of 1979, they had not been able to make a rat move. However, in the '80s, they were successful in moving water from point 'a' to point 'b.'"

7) Aeronautical Systems Center (ASC) at Wright-Patterson is responsible for all the Air Force's black programs including those at Area 51. For instance, the Aurora program is managed by one of ASC's SPO (Systems Program Office) offices: http://www.wpafb.af.mil/asc/

Chapter 2

LOS ALAMOS: LOS ALAMOS NATIONAL LABORATORY (LANL)

In early 1943, J. Robert Oppenheimer, the newly named director of the as-yet-unbuilt nuclear weapons design laboratory at Los Alamos, had to recruit a scientific staff for a purpose he could not disclose, at a place he could not specify, for a period he could not predict. Adding to these ambiguities was the status of the staff; Brig. Gen. Leslie Groves who wanted a military laboratory where scientists served in uniform, a stipulation to which Oppenheimer originally agreed.

Most of the scientists who had been recruited to work on defense projects, however, worked for universities under contract to the Office of Scientific Research and Development (OSRD) and they were reluctant to don uniforms.

In an early recruiting effort, Oppenheimer drafted the team led by Robert Wilson (1), which soon became a research team without a problem, a group with lots of spirit and technique, but nothing to do. Like a bunch of professional soldiers, they signed up, en masse, to go to Los Alamos.

As the troops signed up, Hans Bethe, nuclear physicist (1) at Cornell University, whose summary of nuclear physics in the *Review of Modern Physics*, had become known as the "Bethe Bible," was one such person. He had worked with army officers at MIT on radar projects, and believed that a military regime would be too inflexible for the work at hand.

The challenge of recruiting these senior scientists prepared Oppenheimer for the task of staffing the Laboratory.

So, Oppenheimer armed with the Groves-Conant letter (1) crisscrossed the country adding to his team.

Despite his successes, of the 33 physicists Oppenheimer set out to recruit, only 15 came to Los Alamos. None of these recruits would put on a uniform, and although soldiers would play a role in its work, the laboratory was never militarized.

Groves never again raised the issue of converting the laboratory to a military-style organization. Instead, it was to become an outpost of academia culminating in the explosion of the first atomic bomb at Trinity in 1945.

The transition from war to peace is never easy and that was as true in the case of World War II's "Manhattan Project" as it was for any other aspect of the war. There in New Mexico, the question was how to turn a war-driven, short-term bomb design effort into a stable peacetime operation in charge of producing and maintaining a nuclear stockpile for the nation. Part of J. Robert Oppenheimer's answer to this question was to create Z Division at Los Alamos in July 1945. The "Z Division" was later moved to Sandia base just outside Kirtland AFB and renamed Sandia Laboratory on November 1, 1949, and then became Sandia National Laboratories in 1979 (1) (2). However, recent source information and documents seen in Chapter 3 indicate that there appears to be a Z-Division or Division-Z at LANL that is very much alive and well.

Starting in 1947, Los Alamos figured prominently in the recovery and exploitation of recovered UFOs with a Z-type Division undoubtedly involved in the primary effort since most of the UFO programs were hidden under nuclear weapons programs. The nuclear weapons "cover" was suspected to have been initiated by the National Security Act of 1947, and then supplemented by the Atomic Energy Act of 1954 (See Section 2, Chapter 2, Figure 4). Los Alamos even offered "UFO Crash Recovery" courses in 1954, according to Ed Doty, the uncle of Rick Doty. It is of interest that according to certain MJ-12 documents, both Robert Oppenheimer, former Director of Los Alamos during the Manhattan Project, and Albert Einstein an adviser to the Los Alamos during that time, were contributing members to MAJIC (Military Assessment of the Joint Intelligence Committee) and Majestic-12 or MJ-12 (see Section 1 Chapter 2). Parallel efforts were later reported at Groom Lake and

144

S4 see Section 3, Chapter 4. Black funds were used to support reverse engineering which more than likely came from a number of different agencies like NSA, DIA and CIA.

In the LANL area map (Figure 1), the reader will note areas marked as A, B, and C: These are the areas reported to be the three (3) major underground facilities devoted to study of recovered UFO-alien

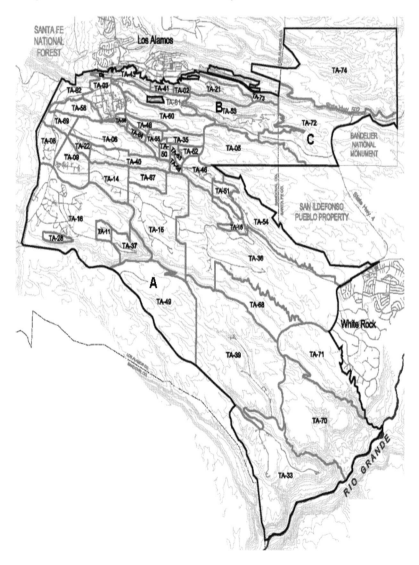

Figure 1

artifacts. The facility marked as "A" is said to be one of the original underground facilities devoted to the study of "alien artifacts" and dates all way back to the early '50s. It was dubbed the "Dulce Complex." If one drives by the front gate of TA 49, you will see that it has a simple fence with a lock on it, nothing unusual (1). Facility "A" was built originally to hold nuclear weapons, but in 1954 it was converted into a complex to study alien artifacts and later used as a "safe-house" for EBE-2.

Nothing is known about Facility "B" but Facility "C" (if these facilities exist at all) is new and reported to be the largest underground facility of its kind in the world with construction starting in 1995 and finishing in 1999. Cost estimates for this "C" facility were said to be over $80 million. It's considered to be "state of the art" in underground construction. The funds for it are suspected to be "black" and stages II and III were finished in the fall of 1999.

Going back to TA 49 or "A" in Figure 1, Building 113 (Figure 2) was reportedly used as one entry way into the TA 49 underground complex, but sources say this entry point was removed a few years ago. Other entries to TA 49 are said to be through TA 33, 36 & 40 where a "side ways" elevator system is used to get from these tech areas to TA 49.

TA 49's public function is known as high explosives (HE) testing area and was the area used to do the conventional high explosives (HE) lens testing for both the Hiroshima and Nagasaki bombs. In 1960 and 1961, a series of experiments involving high explosives and radioactive materials was conducted at the site. These experiments were primarily designed to improve the understanding of certain safety aspects of operational nuclear weapons. Testing continued using low, non-critical amounts of plutonium until the late '60s when it was stopped because of contamination, but conventional HE testing continued (3).

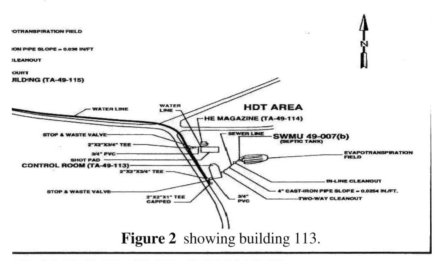

Figure 2 showing building 113.

f TA-49 Septic Systems [(SWMUs 49-007 (a) and (b)].
in engineering drawing ENG-C 44775 .

We have also learned that part of the TA 49 operations could have been moved over to the NTS (Nevada Test Site) underground facility called ENDO-4 instead of moving to facilities "B" or "C" as seen on the LANL tech area map reference Figure1, but this is pure speculation on the part of the sources and could be wrong. As of this writing, we don't know if there is a connection between ENDO-4 and S-4 (see Chapter 4 for S4).

Interview with EBE-2 on March 5th, 1983 at Los Alamos National Labs

"The following is an account of the meeting I, Rick Doty, was involved in with EBE-2.

On March 5, 1983, I was at Los Alamos National Laboratories conducting business on a counterintelligence project. During my visit, a source I'll call 'LANL-1', asked me to sit in on a very special interview. Not knowing what he was talking about, I questioned him. However, he wouldn't say exactly what the project involved or who was being interviewed. I accompanied LANL-1 to an underground facility west of the Los Alamos complex.

The area was called Site 30. Access to this facility was gained by entering Area 49. Access to the underground facility was through building number 49-2091 which is marked as building 113 (entry now closed off) in Figure 2.

An elevator took us down about 60 feet I estimated. Once we arrived, access was gained through a large vault opening outside the elevator. We walked down a hallway to another vault door. We entered and turned right. We walked about 200 feet turned left and entered another vault door to a large room. This room contained two tables, several chairs and recording equipment. I sat near the door. About 10 minutes later, three people, whom I did not know, entered the room. One, an Air Force colonel, asked me to sign a security document, which gave me an upgraded clearance or a TS/SCI/Group-MJ-B-3 clearance. I never heard of this but I signed. The colonel told me I was to listen only and not make any sounds during the interview.

I asked the Colonel who was being interviewed and he told me it was a guest from another planet! The colonel left. The other two people set up a table with a microphone and recording equipment, including a camera. About five minutes later, in walks a 4' 9" nonhuman looking-creature. It was dressed in a tight fitting cream colored suit. It had no hair and was identified to me as EBE-2. EBE-2 sat in a chair across the table from two civilians and the AF colonel. I did not know the identity of the three. LANL-1 came into the room and sat next to me. I listened while the three asked EBE-2 a series of questions pertaining to its home planet. First question was about the temperature, climate and weather. EBE-2 responded in perfect English, but sounded like a machine-generated voice. Very hard to explain but it was either coming from a device that EBE-2 had in front of him or from something in its body (implanted device?). EBE-2 explained the weather of its planet, which was dry, varying temperature between 65-90 degrees. There were 35 hours of constant sunshine and three hours of darkness, the orbital axis is tilted 54 degrees from the vertical to the orbital plane.

Their solar system has 11 planets. Their home planet is the third from the first star or Zeta 1 (this is third party information). The second sun or Zeta 2 lies outside the orbit of the 11th planet. The Jupiter-size planet is the sixth planet. It is 1½ times the size our own Jupiter. [For a report on Zeta Reticuli please see: http://www.ufoconspiracy.com/reports/zetareticuli_star_sys.htm]. Rainfall occurred only during one of its months each year. As mentioned before, a day lasted 38 of our hours. They did not have months but did have years which consisted of approximately 600 of our days (which could mean the planet's orbit is ~1.39 time's further out than the earth's).

They used a "society cycle," which I understood to be similar to our months. During this society cycle, each Eben worked a certain time and conducted business. There was also a rest cycle, which consisted of a regulated period of sleep. I don't recall the exact number of hours for the sleep/rest periods. EBE-2 discussed weather patterns and how they were formed; I don't recall the exact words. However, EBE-2 seemed very intelligent and fully explained each weather pattern in precise detail. He used Earth's equivalents for meteorology terms. The interesting part of this interview was that I didn't hear any questions being asked by the three humans sitting across from EBE-2. Either the questions were already given to EBE-2 or the three humans were "thinking the questions" and EBE-2 would respond in English.

EBE-2 did state his planet's name, but that was in Eben, not English. He never mentioned SERPO (see Section III, Chapter 4, page 189). He also liked the cool climate of Earth around LANL and northern New Mexico and that he was a scientist who was providing assistance to Earth's scientists in the area of space travel.

This interview lasted about one hour. I didn't check my watch, but I estimated from the time I entered the room to the end of the interview was about one hour and 15 minutes. Considering I was in the room about 15 minutes before EBE-2 arrived, I can estimate the interview to have been one hour. When the interview was completed, EBE-2 stood up and walked to the door.

[Rick mentioned that there was also a robot named KOD, which was built based on EBE-2's design. They called it Entity III.]

Just before exiting EBE-2 looked at me, I felt a little strange but I immediately felt happiness! I can't explain it but I just felt really at ease, peaceful. EBE-2 didn't smile but he did make a strange facial expression that I can only assume to be a smile. He then left the room. The colonel then told me I would be escorted out of the facility by LANL-1."

Richard C. Doty

Author comment, EBE-2 had arrived in 1964 and left in 1984 or, approximately two years after this interview.

There are three CIA "leaked" documents (Figures 3, 4, and 5) mentioning EBE-2. These documents are not properly classified instruments. The format is flimsy and they lack certain required classification warning labels and declassification instructions, etc. But as sources tell us these memos were to be read then destroyed. They were not meant to have a long lifetime in the security system. Ernie Kellerstrass and others have stated that the content of the memos are extremely accurate. Rick would say, "I saw these EBE-2 MJ-12 documents in a codeword document published by the Air Force Office of Scientific Intelligence dated in 1985." Dr. Christopher "Kit" Green, Chapter1, would say, "In the years I was there (CIA), they corresponded to the dates on the purported memos."

TOP SECRET

CENTRAL INTELLIGENCE AGENCY
WASHINGTON, D.C. 20505

HANDLE ON STRICT
NEED-TO-KNOW BASIS

May 14, 1980

DCDR5

MA-03

REF: Memo 5-7A

The Texas incident will present a problem for us. Must
determine more info in order to develop dis-info plan.
Why do these things always happen when MJ12 is gone. Luck
is never on our side. Let R-3 know something is up and
that we will need their support to get through this one.

Don't make anymore phone calls on KY3 until the new code is
changed. Too many of the wrong people might be listening.
I don't trust R-2. Could be leak there.

One more thing, EBE-2 has expressed a desire to visit ocean.
I don't know what the hell to do on that one. If we don't
let him, he'll just disappear. Can't allow that to happen
again. MJ6 is working on that. TREAD open/or will be.

MJ9

Figure 3

CENTRAL INTELLIGENCE AGENCY
WASHINGTON, D.C. 20505

June 24, 1982

DCDR2)

NSA/MJ12

Executive Briefing {Memo}

Yesterday R2 requested briefing on Project "A". In particular, he wanted updated info from EBE-2. MJ3 advised that that info was not available to P2. Apparently, White House requested info because of large volume of FOIA requests. Can't seem to make those fools realize EBE-2 info is not available for any dissemination, per EO 01156, regardless of who requests info. Contact T-2P and see if he can assume custody of the matter.

Don't allow AF to evaluate IDENT info. They may open up a little too much. KEND-3 can assist to some extent.

MJ5.

TOP SECRET

Figure 4

TOP SECRET

CENTRAL INTELLIGENCE AGENCY

WASHINGTON, D.C. 20505

December 28, 1982

DCDR-3/55

MJ12

REF: TA Memo 3-20

TR-3 related both phases of OP-KIWI compromised by leak. Terminate phase I and re-direct energy to dis-info. EBE-2 can't be located at this time. R4 has placed him in safehouse somewhere near Edwards. I don't even know the exact location. No transfer will be approved until Phase I in DP23. CAP-3 not ready to receive EBE-2. Don't even know if they have facilities available for holding. CLASS YY-II only available at Kirtland or Los Alamos. Must make decision before Jan 15. No other options open.

NORAD not cooperating with MJ4 on D-SITE studies. We may have to contact KERW-302 personnel and have them conduct study. NORAD still operating on old system. The big problem is only a few of NORAD's personnel are clear for SONG-DANCE info.

PETE-23 open class II. REPEAT BLOCK NOT USED. DON'T NEGLECT MAKING CHANGES TO BOTH BLOCKS. CODES EXPIRE ON 31 DEC.

MJ5

TOP SECRET

HANDLE ON STRICT
NEED-TO-KNOW BASIS

Figure 5

I not only saw often and used the rather odd stationary for my own internal memos, but for the same "kind of" internal memo-routing. The form of type-font–a little eclectic to say the least–I had also seen from the CIA/DDO. And, it is true also–that I never saw those memos or any others on the (UFO) subject. I also noted however, that references to "IDENT" were correct, in they referred to a U.S. subject DCD-type sourcing."

Partial list of "Terms" used in the three (3) MJ-12 EBE-2 memos

• TREAD: Transmitted Encrypted Analysis Data;

• IDENT info: CIA term to mean identification of information accomplished;

• KEND-3: CIA term for special secure communication phone;

• OP-KIWI: CIA operation involving EBE-2;

• Song-Dance: Disinformation program to hide truth about EBE-2;

• Class YY-II: Has been identified as an EBE holding facility;

• Sources can't identify EO 01156;

• D-Site, KERW-302 (but could be a coded message system used by CIA), PETE-23;

• SID (might mean Scientific Intelligence Division), SI-3-TR-WE-EO or 24 Class;

• R2 is Bush 1 according to Bill Moore.

We have focused on facilities in this chapter versus the personalities because of an almost complete lack of knowledge of how the players might have interacted on a day-to-day basis in the MJ-12 arena.

Secrecy was the order of the day. As we saw with TA 49 (HE Testing), facilities were used as covers to support covert UFO operations. Dulce was said to have over a hundred rooms covering five (5) levels (ground level is Level 1) with each level being over a football field in length. We can only imagine the enormous amount of black funds used to build facilities like Dulce even in 1954 dollars.

Reverse engineering is at the heart of what this book is about, so if a UFO did crash at Roswell and other places what did they do with all that hardware besides what we already know? Why hasn't reverse engineering moved more quickly? Why are there so many problems, yet so few solutions? We will attempt to answer those and many other questions in the coming chapters.

References/Footnotes

(1) History of LANL: How did the Laboratory come to be located in Los Alamos? Who were the movers and shakers who created it? And, how did a small group of people transplanted to a tiny, isolated community in the mountains of northern New Mexico conceive of a weapon that would forever change history? http://www.lanl.gov/history/road/milit-lab.shtml

(2) *End of a War: Beginning of a Laboratory, Z DIVISION 1945-1949*, http://www.sandia.gov/recordsmgmt/zdiv.html.

(3) Overhead of TA 49, seven kilometers south of Los Alamos, New Mexico, http://terraserver.microsoft.com/ image.aspx?t=1&s=10&x=1914&y=19830&z=13&w=1

Chapter 3

LOS ALAMOS NATIONAL LAB (LANL), REVERSE ENGINEERING

Did some of the correspondence or documents on the following pages reportedly come from a "non-existent" LANL Z-Division? (1)

Is it the same Z-Division that Robert Oppenheimer (referenced in last chapter) established in July 1945 and which was an operation that was in charge of producing and maintaining a nuclear stockpile for the nation? (Named after Jerrold Zacharia, http://mfnl.xjtu.edu.cn/gov-doe-sandia/50years/answers1-19-98/answer3c.htm). This was the same Z-Division that was moved to the Sandia base outside of Albuquerque and later officially renamed Sandia Laboratory on November 1, 1949, and Sandia National Laboratories in 1979, as mentioned in last Chapter (2). But, in the classified world, Z-Division perhaps never really left LANL and is still very much alive and well. This is from source information and declassified UFO documents with the word "Restricted" stamped on them. We know that many of the more "sensitive" UFO secrets were kept buried under nuclear weapons programs as mentioned in the previous chapters (See Section 2, Chapter 2, Figure 4 where the Atomic Energy Act of 1954 is mentioned in connection with UFOs).

So, by extension, we can surmise from both the MJ-12 and recent DIA (Defense Intelligence Agency, Figures 2 and 3) leaked documents that a non-existent LANL Z-Division had played a highly significant role on the subject of UFOs since 1947.

The author doesn't pretend to fully understand all the supposed confidential material that has been sent to him. We present this material here in the hopes that further research by us and others will yield better results. We begin with the document in Figures 1a, b, c which are raw scientific notes for Eben craft number 2 reported

These notes pertain to the Eben Craft Number 2.

>>

While electric charges cannot be conducted from the charge-accumulating fluid directly through the toroid walls and edges there will be a capacitive effect which will accumulate charges of an opposite polarity, on the outside surfaces which will correspond to the inner ones in intensity and location. This "diffuse layer", as its called, of electric charge, occurs most effectively when the liquid(e-plasma), is moving, and the faster the e-plasma moves the more pronounced will be the separation effect of its electric ions from the ions in the differently moving diffused layer outside.

In this respect the charges that accumulate outside in the space around the lower inner edge of the toroid in its diffuse layer, that encircles the base disc assembly, would be negative. And the charges accumulating around the outside of the whole of the outer circumference of the toroid would be positive. The result being much the same as dipolar electrodes - building up between them electrostatic field lines and potential magnetic field around those lines.

Inside the craft, over the top horizontal plane of the toroid, which also forms the lower face of the radial planar guide, the induced electrical charges react with toroid's magnetic field so as to form a horizontally rotating field of polarized (positive) ions. This revolving positive field reacts with the normal air outside the craft to initiate an inflowing of polarized and neutrally charged air which, as soon as it passes through the craft's circumferential duct and over the toroid's electrically-charged outer edge, becomes positively ionized from the effect of sharp-edge ionization. When the inflowing air passes through the duct its specially designed curved surface acts as a constrictor to speed up the air flow thereby creating a low pressure area inside the duct.

The increase in the circumferential duct's peripheral potential correspondingly increases the oppositely-charged potential of the fluid on the inside of the toroid.

When the magnetic fields begin to resonate the flux lines will create electrical eddy currents over the under-face of the floor surface, so that a skin of charged particles will circulate around the surface. The base can be capacitively coupled to the upper outside dome-shell of the craft so as to enable the metallic dome to acquire an outside positive charge. The dome itself can be made to store a tremendous amount

Figure 1a

of electrical energy, over it's whole surface area, if it is structured as a capacitor.

The central rotating assembly is made up of four bi-polar sphere-sets held equally spaced in a metallic plate. The plate is formed in such a way as to fit inside the perimeter of the inner lower edge of the toroid, so as to be able to rotate freely with the sphere-set, but to also form an electrostatic coupling with the charges on the lower edge of the toroid. This base plate also has a small diameter emission hole at its center.

The base plates, as well as holding the four bi-poles, has to impede and constrict the lower magnetic field of the toroid, so as to direct the flux lines through, or mainly through, its central hole. This then, would not be made of the same construction as the toroid shell and would be made of a non-magnetic metal (similar to the magnesium/bismuth/zinc like material found in Roswell Number 1)on the lower plates. This base plate material is similar to the Roswell Number 1 material but differs in composition since it contains an aluminum like substance as the bonding agent. The base plate must contain some bismuth, since bismuth does have a sort of qualities needed as it does exhibit what is called "lag current" when pulsed currents are applied to it at a very low frequencies (2mhz to 8 mhz) and in a strong magnetic field indicating that it has capacitance. Bismuth also has a high atomic mass and of course a Hall effect resistance or diamagnetism. Either way, a non-magnetic material while not able to prevent all magnetic flux lines from penetrating through it, will convert some of the flux to a rotating electric field (eddy currents) over it surfaces which will supplement the action of other charged particles spinning around the large lower spheres by other interactions, and these rotations will coalesce into a flux-constricting force. The base plate metal could also be laminated on its outside with some sort of insulating material that has not been found.

During recent tests, it was determined that Eben 1! Sent out an electronic signature of super-high radio-frequency electromagnetic pulses. The pulses are in the 3 Ghz region of the electromagnetic spectrum at a wavelength of 1- centimeters. Because the waves are so short and their frequency is so high the normal sort of capacitance-inductance oscillator with its conductor/antenna emission systems can't cope and so different sort of electronics technology is needed to radiate these waves out of the craft and into the air or space around it. There are various methods of doing this with short "millimeter" waves, one of which is called the transmission line, another is with the parabolic antenna and another is the waveguide. Of these three of the best suited systems for propagated electric field propulsion is the waveguide, which basically, is a rectangular metal tube whereby at one end the microwave power is

Figure 1b

pumped in, and at the other end the delivery of these power waves occurs with almost undiminished intensity. The science of waveguides is quite fascinating and is nothing like cable or conductor type electronics, the size and the very shape of a waveguide computes in an entirely different fashion toward the end result. Microwaves though are a very useful range of frequencies; at one particular frequency (3 GHz for atmospheric air) they can then create spin-resonance in the electrons of atoms of the gases in the surrounding air, Electron spin resonance-ESR raises the normal mode "lower" energy" state of the electron up to the higher energy state, the visual effect of which is an emission of light photons of various colors (the subject of which is already covered in LANL-Z Alpha Report 0/23-0091).

Figure 1c

by the LANL-Z Alpha Team. The sources fully admit they don't understand how the craft really work.

Even those PhDs in Zero Point Energy and quantum physics like H. E. Puthoff of the Institute of Advanced Studies, Austin, TX, don't fully understand what these notes are really saying (see references on H. E. Puthoff, Section 1, Chapter 1). Also, references to Eben1 in the notes means Eben craft #1; and see next discussion on what these notes might mean.

Those "Dumb" Questions

"Greetings Charles, reference that e-mail you sent to my source well, I'm one of those dumb friends. You're right we don't have much of a clue about how our ET craft work except for saying it might be anti-gravity. From reading that document several times (Figure 1), I think I can say that you wrote that for a selected audience or those with a background and having current or prior tickets, us dummies have not been so fortunate. So, if you don't mind, I'd like to ask a few questions that hopefully might clarify things for us less fortunate if you don't mind?"

1) In one case you mention: "liquid (e-plasma)."

Question: Is this "e-plasma" super-conducting and composed of "Cooper Pairs?"

2) You say, "magnetic fields begin to resonate."

Question: Resonate how?

3) You state: "The base can be capacitively coupled to the upper-outside dome-shell of the craft to enable the metallic dome to acquire an outside positive charge. The dome itself can be made to store a tremendous amount of electrical energy, over its whole surface area, if it is structured as a capacitor."

Question: Isn't the whole craft considered one big capacitor?

4) You state: "which will supplement the action of other charged particles spinning around the large lower spheres by other interactions, and these rotations will coalesce into a flux-constricting force."

Question: Please explain, "other interactions" and, what is the nature of this "flux-constricting force?"

There are many more questions, but for now I'd hope you consider answering the above. Thanks in advance.

Regards,

Robert Collins

Charles (LANL Source) then writes on 01-04-04:

"Before answering your questions, you are assuming that ET crafts are made with our technology based on your questions. Many years ago, we made that same mistake and it took us several years to correct the mistake and start fresh from the drawing board. "Their" technology is nothing similar to ours. We do not utilize our physics or chemistry in a comparison analysis. We started from scratch and learned their principles of dynamics, physics, etc.

"The document (Figure 1) I gave my contact was a briefing to people with some basic knowledge of the craft. I used our grammar and basic English comparison phrases to explain a very complex ET system.

"The ET craft was manufactured using ET technology. This craft was built many years before we developed flight. They used a different physics principle that we still don't fully understand. We cannot duplicate the craft's material. We have nothing similar to that material on Earth. We have similar substances, metals, etc, but 80% of the craft's outer shell is made of an unknown type of material that we do not have on Earth. Some of it is made from a substance similar to Zinc but with a different atomic weight and valence.

"The primary propulsion system is electro-magnetic flux directional positive force (meant negative force?) generating system. The secondary propulsion system is an anti-gravity (using fluid plasma) directional negative force generating system. Remember, these are our terms. The entire craft can be a super conductor or a super capacitor depending on how the propulsion system is configured. Like I said, the system is extremely complicated. Unless you understand the entire system, which we don't, you won't understand what I am saying.

"The electrical system works on a vacuum vacated energy principle. This system generates an unlimited amount of power. The Visitors have determined that hydrogen has many more isotopes than we thought. H5 is one isotope they harness and use as a catalyst inside the power device.

Author's comments: For "our" H5 see (5).

"Getting to your questions, it would do you no good for me to answer those questions. You would be completely baffled by my answers. It is best to let the questions sit until the completed information is made public.

"I directed no disrespect to your regarding the "dumb friends" statement. I simply meant people without the inside knowledge makes statements that are dumb. I've worked on this project for 12 years and I sometimes call myself dumb because I try to compare the craft with our technology. Doing that is dumb, as all who have worked on the craft over the years have come to understand."

Regards,

Charles, LANL contact

Another contact by the name of Gene Lakes known as Gene Loscowski (Chapter 4, p. 186) concurs with the LANL source. The e-mail is dated September 15th, 2005.

"You are relating our physics to their crafts—can't do that. That was our mistake for many years. To get into outer space, they use THEIR system. To understand THEIR system, you must understand their physics, which, at least during my time, we had problems with. It was explained to me this way. Our gravity theories evolved from Newton. But their gravity applications are not consistent with Newton Laws of Physics. We spent many years applying Newton's Laws of Physics to their craft–guess what–they didn't apply. Once we started to use their applications (given to us by a friend), we started understanding their systems. You are correct in the mentioning Negative Force Generator (NFG) and Negative Curvature Field System (NCFS). They are descriptions I heard. But I never heard of antigravity. So, I guess some of the information provided to you by those LANL sources is correct...Gene."

James Jesus Angleton's Einstein's Notes from 1951-'52?

Below is an extract taken from the hundreds of personal hand written notes taken during classified CIA briefings which belonged to James

J. Angleton who was fired/retired from the CIA in 1974 (see, Section II Chapter 1). Graciously, the grandson James Angleton provided many of the notes to these authors. It must be emphasized that JJA was not a technical person so the notes are sketchy and unclear in many cases. The reason for presenting this extract is to show readers the similarity between what the Los Alamos source was saying and what these "Einstein notes" say; example, that the craft(s) can be considered as one big super-conducting capacitor, etc. The notes go on to mention electron pairs and other technical issues. But, the BCS (Bardeen, Cooper and Schrieffer) (2) theory of electron pairs called Cooper pairs was not published until 1957. So how can this extract be real? The one redeeming quality is that it mentions "electron pairs" not "Cooper pairs."

"The qualitative picture is a local field of positive cosmological constants contributing to the local metric field in a small boundary layer around the skin of the craft. The layer was controlled by the EM brainwave of the pilot. The pilot also has a Q* type of field. Dr Einstein expanded…. The fuselage of the craft was more liken to a high temperature super-conductor to which the occupants do not feel the g forces at high accelerations or sharp turns. There is a direct correlation to mind-linkage via headband and hand-panels. There is an exotic field surrounding the vehicle. The hull had super-conducting properties. We watched the craft displace gravity via propagation by a magnetic wave (3). It resonated at first, ALF (Alien Life Form) our liaison, telepathically explained its basic propulsion stating that "N" in the equation (not shown) is the number of pairs in the super-conductor (these electron pairs contribute to the anti-gravity effect)…with a slowly changing component and frequency for the EM field." This statement is followed by numerous equations.

This scene seems to be depicted in the 1951 movie, "The Day the Day Earth Stood Still" (4) where in this case the scientist is Albert Einstein and the alien is ALF.

It continues: "Once our pilots understood the interaction of the craft, they were not affected by the g-forces and that under tremendous acceleration the craft bent gravity or folded it around the outer hull of the craft. The pilots claimed they knew they were going very fast, but it was so fast that they saw things stand still in time. The bow and stern warped under dynamic action. At first our pilots could not interface with the craft. ALF corrected the problem by assisting the interface with 3 fingers on the globe panel then the wave formed and the craft begun to cooperate and generate lift. They also had to use the smallest pilots under 5ft 3 inches to wear the headband and garb, which also helped in g-force displacement.

Encrypted was following: 0800/23/6/52/EODCI/DSC/OSI/E"

Is anti-gravity real? Did Albert Einstein really start the whole reverse engineering process right after Roswell which continues to this day? Paper evidence says "yes" but that never really satisfies anyone. Where do we go from here? Let's try an energy device.

Alien Energy Device (ED), Code Named Crystal Rectangle and H5 Production?

An alien energy device (ED) code named "Crystal Rectangle?" This code name is not shown on the documents. Some sources specifically, a retired chief of security at Area 51 informed this author in September 2005 that the content of the documents are real, but the documents are not; i.e., the serial numbers and code words could not be authenticated by the DIA office at Los Alamos. However, is the DIA office lying in the interest of National Security? Figures 2, 3, 4, 5 and 6 are depicted followed by a strenuous effort by these authors to offer some rational explanations. Both Richard Helms (ex CIA Director and friend of the Doty family) and Tom Mack (retired AF major and friend of Rick Doty) mentioned this CR device before they died. Richard Helms is quoted in 1999 as stating:"It was later learned that the communication device was connected to the CR by a small glass tube (fiber optics?), (footnote 6, Chapter 3). There were no wires within this glass tube (more like a crystal-type material)."

Tom Mack (Chapter 4, reference 12) would say in a personal e-mail to this author, "CR was the code for, Crystal Rectangle, which was the material and shape of the device. It could generate a large amount of energy, however we never could duplicate it and could not understand how it worked. We couldn't make hydrogen 5 in large quantities; in fact, we made a small amount but it dissipated in a matter of nano-seconds. We had no way of making it and storing it (5). To the best of my knowledge, the CR is still stored underground at LANL."

Figure 2 says, "The material contained in this report was received from the Scientific Advisory Group, Special Mission Section, Los Alamos National Laboratories, Los Alamos, NM."

It states: "During a recovery mission of an extraterrestrial space craft in Jun 1947, several pieces of debris were found. It further says, "Further analysis by Dr. Edward Teller, revealed the debris to be an energy device (ED)." The ED uses Hydrogen 5 (H5) as a catalyst to extract energy from the vacuum as explained below.

"The interior of the device contained six thousand three hundred and sixty-six (6,366) small black circular objects (.003 cm) that spins clockwise within a circular sphere filled with liquid when a demand of electricity is placed on the device. The black object apparently aggravates a liquid material, believed to be an isotope of hydrogen. The process produces a displacement of energy inside the device that is directed to the export tubes. The hydrogen isotope was identified as an isotope similar to Tritium however, this liquid has four neutrons."

As it states in the document, our scientists as of 1995 had no idea how this device really worked except for knowing the role H5 might play. However, in 2001 and later, concerted efforts were being made to fly this device on selected space shuttle missions and the space station. At the same time Los Alamos was making concerted attempts in reverse engineering (please see Figures again).

The Figure 3 document shows repeated attempts to test the alien energy device (ED) on board the shuttle and International Space Station with phenomenal results for its small size and weight. Supposedly, the ED was used to power equipment during the construction of the International Space Station. It supplied voltage from 9 volts/.5 amperes to 1100 volts/100 amperes where the demand did not cause heat buildup or electro magnetic induction (EMI). At no time, as the document says, did the ED cause any problems with measuring equipment or avionics on board the space

---

DEFENSE INTELLIGENCE AGENCY
SCIENTIFIC INTELLIGENCE REPORT

CLASSIFICATION: **TOP SECRET**   **CODEWORD:** POP STRIKE

NOTE: This document contains information affecting the national defense of the United States within the meaning of the espionage laws, Title 18, U.S.C., 793 and 979. The transmission of the contents in any manner by unauthorized person is prohibited by law.

TOP SECRET CONTROL NR: 95-T3-034-E   **DATE:** 11 JUN 95

---

1. **SUBJECT:** (TS) Extraterrestrial Energy Device   2. **REPORT NUMBER:** (S) 00001/CE/54

3. **NSO NUMBER:** 95-16   4. **ORIGINATOR:** (S) SPECIAL CAT-K

5. **PREPARED BY:** JANET CASSIDY, GS-14   6. **REPORT DATE:** 11 JUN 95
                  TI Advisory Group

SUMMARY:

(TS) The material contained in this report was received from the Scientific Advisory Group, Special Mission Section, Los Alamos National Laboratories, Los Alamos, NM.

(TS) During a recovery mission of an extraterrestrial space craft in Jun 1947, several pieces of debris were found. During scientific experiments of this debris, one piece displayed unusual characteristics. Further analysis by Dr. Edward Teller, revealed the debris to be an energy device (ED). From 1957 until present, the ED has undergone a variety of tests. Each test revealed non-earthly abilities of the ED. The ED was placed under the controls of the Special Mission Section of the Scientific Advisory Group, Defense Intelligence Agency. As of today, the ED has not been disclosed to non senior Defense Department Personnel.

ED CHARACTERISTICS:

(U) The following characteristics are provided for the ED:

(TS) Weight: 41.4 oz   Dimensions: 8.24 inches wide, 11.65 inches tall, 2.8 inches thick.

(TS) Description: The exterior is made of a hard plastic type material. The material contains carbon, nickel, zinc, bismuth, magnesium and several unknown elements and/or materials. Two black electricity export tubes are located on the upper right and lower left corner of the device. A small black square, 2 cm by 2 cm, is located on the lower left area of the device. Under high magnification, the interior of this square appears to be similar to a computer chip. Electron mapping of this square was completed. The interior of the device contained six thousand, three hundred and sixty-six small black circular objects (.003 cm) that spins clockwise within a circular sphere filled with liquid when a demand of electricity is placed on the device. The black object apparently aggravates a liquid material, believed to be an isotope of hydrogen. The process produces a displacement of energy inside the device that is directed to the export tubes. The hydrogen isotope was identified as an isotope similar to Tritium, however, this liquid has four neutrons. We have been unable to understand the chemical principles displayed by this device. The small black "chip" located in the lower left corner, may be the control mechanism for this device.

TOP SECRET

Figure 2a: DIA TS/Pop Strike document.

DEFENSE INTELLIGENCE AGENCY
SCIENTIFIC INTELLIGENCE REPORT

continuation sheet

TOP SECRET

(TS) However, the intricate pattern of this chip cannot be understood. It does not appear to be of a design known to our scientific community.

(TS) The electrical output of the ED varies from one millivolt to megavolts. The ED seems to sense the demand placed upon it and then generates the exact amount of electricity to satisfy the demand. The electrical output characteristics of the ED cannot be understood. The electrical patterns displayed on an oscilloscope is unknown to our technology. The displayed patterns does not coincide with our technology, however, the electrical output is exactly the correct waves to satisfy the demand.

(TS) 165 scientific experiments have been performed on the ED during the last 40 years. The conclusion of the scientific advisory board of scientists is that the ED is too advanced for the scientific understanding of the 20th century technology.

CONCLUSION:

(TS) We have not been able to duplicate the ED. The materials contained in the ED cannot be duplicated by our technology. The ED has been transported to several national laboratories for evaluation. The ED will be transported to a secure location and stored until further advances in our technology allows for experimentation.

DISTRIBUTION BY ORIGINATOR:

SPECIAL DISTRIBUTION CAT-JAVA
SIMBER-GRAY WORKING GROUP

DOWNGRADING: BY ORIGINATOR

TOP SECRET

Figure 2b: DIA TS/Pop Strike document.

station. In further reading we see terms like "Lorentz force," "Hall effect" and the Van der Pauw effect. Please see: http://www.eeel.nist.gov/812/effe.htm for explanations of those terms .

DEFENSE INTELLIGENCE AGENCY
SCIENTIFIC INTELLIGENCE REPORT

CLASSIFICATION: TOP SECRET   **CODEWORD:** ARC WELD

NOTE: This document contains information affecting the national defense of the United States within the meaning of the espionage laws, Title 18, U.S.C., 793 and 979. The transmission of the contents in any manner by unauthorized person is prohibited by law.

TOP SECRET CONTROL NR: 01-04-2231-TI   **DATE:** 19 APR 2001

1. **SUBJECT:** (TS) PHYSICAL EFFECTS ON ENERGY DEVICE(ED) DURING SPACE SHUTTLE MISSIONS

2. **REPORT NUMBER:** (S) 1010/01/TI-3

3. **NSO NUMBER:** (U)01-23   4. **ORIGINATOR:** (S) SPECIAL CAT-K

5. **PREPARED BY:** (S) DR. KENNETH GISH, TI Advisory Group   6. **REPORT DATE:** (U)19 APR 01

7. **CLASSIFICATION:** (U) BY DIA/CC-4 EXEMPT UNDER 12958
   SENSITIVE COMPARTMENTAL INFORMATION: (S) TK/OKAT

SUMMARY:

(TS/TK) The ED was transported to space by STS-92, October 11, 2000, STS-97, November 30, 2000 and STS-106, September 8, 2000. Sixteen experiments were conducted using the ED in space. All experiments involved the use of high voltage/high amperes and low voltage/low amperes powered by the ED.

(TS/TK) The results of these experiments showed the ED could be used to power all systems onboard a space shuttle and the International Space Station.

DETAILS:

(TS/TK) TI Advisory Group-6 was asked to loan the ED to NASA in order to conduct voltage/amperes experiments in space. The ED was flown onboard the space shuttle during three missions (STS-92, STS-97, STS-106). During these flights, the ED was under complete military control by cleared personnel (William McArthur, STS-92 and Joseph Tanner, STS-97 and Terry Wilcutt, STS-106). The ED was used to power equipment used during the construction of the International Space Station. The ED supplied voltage from 9 volts/.5 amperes to 1100 volts/100 amperes. Demand on the ED did not cause heat build up or electro magnetic induction(EMI). EMI rates were non measurable during the tests. During one experiment (STS-92 involving SIMS arcing) the ED did not show any measurable EMI or electro magnetic arcing. The ED varied in weigh from 693 grams to 705 grams during demand tests. Aggravating of internal components did not cause undue heat measurements. The measurable heat range during the experiments were recorded at .008C from the high voltage/amperes output to .004C to the low voltage/amperes output. The ED and its application harness were the only equipment used during these experiments. At no time did the demand on the ED cause any problems with measuring equipment or avionics on board the space shuttle.

Figure 3a: DIA TS/Arc Weld document.

DEFENSE INTELLIGENCE AGENCY
SCIENTIFIC INTELLIGENCE REPORT

continuation sheet

Report Nr: 1010/01/TI-3	TOP SECRET	Date: 19 Apr 01

(TS/TK) Normally, electrons subject to the Lorentz force, drift away from the electrical current line towards the negative source resulting in an excess surface electrical charge on the output loop. Within the ED, this did not occur. Within the ED, at least during zero gravity study, electrons seem to defy the Lorentz force. No measurable EMI was detected on or around the ED. The Hall effect did not exist. There was no voltage drop across the two port output terminals of the ED. The sheet density on the ED was measured at less than 30 coulombs, which is not significant. No Van der Pauw effect to the resistivity of the ED was measured. At the point of demand, the Lattice seemed to move counterclockwise within the internal circular armature. The Boson spin of the aggravated particles within the Armature was also counterclockwise during zero gravity. The Theta angle of the EMI was > 90 degrees during high voltage output. During low voltage output, the Theta angle could not be measured. Comparison ratios of different scientific effects must be conducted between zero gravity and positive gravity. Lenz law seems to vary with the amount of demand placed on the ED. The input flux produced by the induced electrical current was opposite that of the output flux measured at the output port of the ED.

CONCLUSION:

(TS/TK) The ED showed remarkable power output during these experiments. No problems were encountered and no false measurements or false avionics readings were recorded. The ED showed it could supple any amount of voltage/amperes that was placed upon the device. The ED defied standard scientific principles and laws during the zero gravity tests. TI Advisory Group plans the use of the ED on future space shuttle flights. The ED will fly on board STS-100, 107, 108, 114 and 115.

DISTRIBUTION BY ORIGINATOR:

(S) SPECIAL DISTRIBUTION CAT-K	Cy 23 of 30
(S) SIMBER-GRAY VICTOR DIVISION	
(TS/RD) LANL/DIVISION-Z10	

DOWNGRADING: BY ORIGINATOR
EXEMPTION-M

Figure 3b: DIA TS/Arc Weld document.

A few added comments about Figure 3: TS/TK means "Top Secret Talent Keyhole" data. Talent Keyhole was used to protect sensitive data obtained from spy satellites. The three astronauts mentioned in the Figure 3 document are real; please see reference 6. Also, note the grammar erros in Figures 2b and 3b with the mixing of plural with singular and the word "supply" spelled as "supple." These grammar errors are used to track sensitive documents.

The magnetic flux chamber in Figure 4 is used to harness the energy created by the alien energy device or ED (reference the DIA documents in Figures 2 and 3) or it might be used to harness energy from our own reverse engineered ED (reference Figure 6). No comment or explanation from the LANL source on how this really works other than what is seen in the drawing.

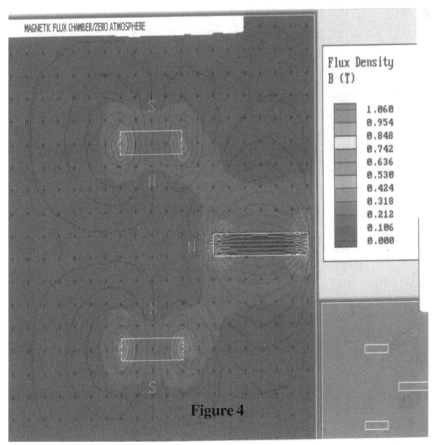

Figure 4

Figures 5 and 6 depict LANL's attempts at producing H5 and then designing an energy device (ED) supposedly based on the alien design, but using our own technology. Again, no explanation from sources as to how these devices might work other than what is seen in the drawings.

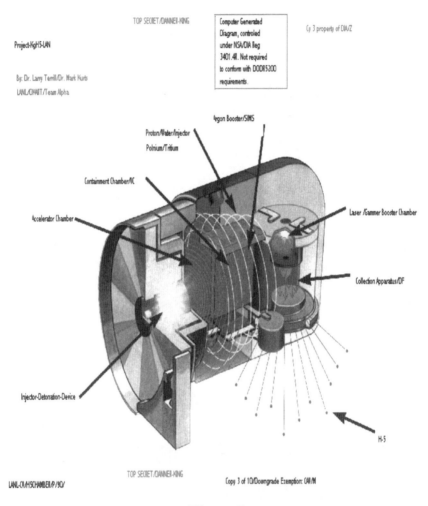

Figure 5

Figure 5 is a computer-generated diagram for H5 production at LANL classified "TOP SECRET/DANNER-KING" controlled under NSA/DIA Reg 3401.4R. Diagram is by Dr. Larry Terrill and Dr. Mark Kurts LANL/ OKART/Team Alpha. This is the same Alpha Team who did the Eben # 2 craft report shown in Figure 1. Note again the grammar errors which are typical of internal documents and it is those same grammar errors whch [sic] are used to track sensitive documents as mentioned earlier.

There is something called a "KIM design" which is reportedly a patented design created by LANL to store certain chemicals in a stable state. Sources stated that H5 is stored in a special container under a special method involving the KIM. Previously, in Figures 2 and 3 we saw that the aliens reportedly used a "crystal rectangle" or "ED" to store H5 in a stable state. In Figure 6 is an energy device (ED) diagram from the same LANL confidential source.

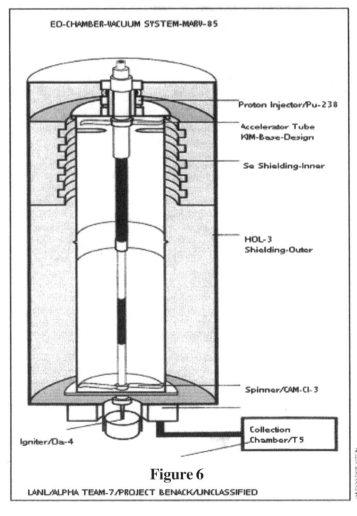

Figure 6

LANL/ALPHA TEAM-7/PROJECT BENACK/UNCLASSIFIED

This reportedly represents LANL's attempts to reverse engineer the alien ED device as described in the DIA TS/Codeword documents. There are very few details available on this device and most of the questions were answered with, "That's classified." As mentioned earlier, we believe this device makes use of H5 which is then used as a catalyst to extract energy from the vacuum thereby providing an energy output for the ED (The H5 very unstable, but reportedly not for Alpha Team 7). The KIM-based design, as noted before, is a patented design created by LANL to store certain chemicals in a stable base. Regarding HOL-3, our source wouldn't say, and added it was highly classified and the same for Da-4, or classified.

The Cash-Landrum Case Revisited

Figure 7: Artist James Neff's rendition of the Cash-Landrum incident.

In December 1980, Betty Cash, Vickie Landrum and her grandson Colby Landrum, were driving along a road in Huffman, TX, when they saw a bright light in the sky. After driving a little more along the road, they came across a large diamond shaped UFO hovering over the road belching fire out of the bottom. Since the flames were blocking the road, they had to stop the car about 65 yards away from the craft and the three of them got out. Vickie and Colby stayed by the car while Betty went on to get a closer look. She spent a long time gazing at it, but then her skin began to burn because of the heat from the flames (Heat and flames generated by an air-cooled nuclear reactor and/or Doppler shifting of the radiation due to the anti-gravity field?). She returned to the car as the object began to rise and then a large number of unmarked black helicopters chased after the UFO. Many more helicopters later joined the UFO. When they got home, they started suffering from sunburn, diarrhea and vomiting.

Rick Doty and others have stated that the Cash-Landrum (CL) case of December 29, 1980 was one of our reverse-engineered craft gone out of control (7). From what has been learned it seems this craft was a very primitive attempt by the US government to find a fast track, secret way to get us into space and off to the stars using anti-gravity as the propulsion mechanism (part of Project Snowbird?). But, according to the LANL contact, nothing work and they had to start all over again. As the contact had said, there were problems with the materials, propulsion system, and understanding the alien's power system. Edward Teller had supposedly identified the power system as far back as 1957. But as to how it really works–other than the use of H5– is still a mystery according to that DIA document in Figure 2.

According to certain sources there is a top secret astronaut corps at Area 51 who fly these reverse-engineered craft. Donald Rumsfeld who is a former Naval Aviator has a reported keen interest in this corps.

The story these documents and drawings tell is stunning and shocking if true. We have no way of verifying much of this material except for the shuttle astronauts. Because so much of the material appears to remain highly classified and sensitive, it is extremely hard for these authors to explain much more than what has been presented. From what we are hearing it would take an "act of god" to force the government to declassify anything like what the readers have learned in this chapter.

Having focused here, let us pursue the ideas of reverse-engineering even further by venturing out to Area 51-S4 and attempt to separate fact from fiction.

References/Footnotes

(1) *End of a War: Beginning of a Laboratory, Z DIVISION,* 1945-1949: http://www.sandia.gov/recordsmgmt/zdiv.html#zdiv_3

(2) BCS (Bardeen, Cooper, and Schrieffer) theory of electron pairs: http://en.wikipedia.org/wiki/Cooper_pairComments

(3) "Experimental Detection of the Gravitomagnetic London Moment," 2006. By--Martin Tajmar1, Florin Plesescu, Klaus Marhold & Clovis J. de Matos.

(4) "The Day the Earth Stood Still:" http://en.wikipedia.org/wiki/The_Day_the_Earth_Stood_Still .

(5) http://physicsweb.org/article/news/5/8/15 "A super heavy isotope of hydrogen that has four neutrons and a proton in its nucleus has been detected for the first time. Physicists have been attempting to create hydrogen-5–which is thought to exist inside stars–for over 40 years."

(6) List of astronauts on the shuttle fights, http://www.jsc.nasa.gov/Bios/htmlbios/mcarthur.html , http://www.jsc.nasa.gov/Bios/htmlbios/tanner.html , http://www.jsc.nasa.gov/Bios/htmlbios/wilcutt.html.

(7) "Diamond in the Sky: The Betty Cash and Vickie Landrum," December 29, 1980 UFO incident at, http://ufos.about.com/library/weekly/aa091498.htm.

Chapter 4

AREA 51 (WATERTOWN, THE RANCH), S4 (SHADY REST, THE DESERT DISNEYLAND)

A Secret Desert Mythology

According to the conventional history, the origin of the Groom Lake test facility can be traced to the Central Intelligence Agency's Project "AQUATONE" that encompassed the development of the Lockheed U-2 (1). It was capable of flying at high altitudes while carrying sophisticated cameras and sensors; the U-2 was equipped with a single jet engine and long, tapered straight wings. The CIA did not want to test fly the new aircraft at Edwards AFB or Palmdale (A.F. Plant 42) in California. For security reasons, a more remote site was required. At the request of U-2 designer Clarence L. "Kelly" Johnson of Lockheed Skunk Works, project pilot Tony LeVier scouted numerous locations around the southwestern United States for a new test site. The other rumored reason, not officially acknowledged, was to eventually test and fly recovered alien craft,

Richard M. Bissell Jr., who was director of the AQUATONE program, reviewed 50 potential sites with his Air Force liaison, Col. Osmond J. "Ozzie" Ritland. None of the sites seemed to meet the stringent security requirements of the program. Ritland, however, recalled "a little X-shaped field" in southern Nevada that he had flown over many times during his involvement with nuclear weapons tests. The airstrip, called Nellis auxiliary field No.1, was located just off the eastern side of Groom Dry Lake, about 100 miles north of Las Vegas. It was also just outside the Atomic Energy Commission's (AEC) nuclear proving ground at Yucca Flat.

In April 1955, LeVier, Johnson, Bissell, and Ritland flew to Nevada on a two-day survey of the most promising lake beds. After examining Groom Lake, it was obvious that this was an ideal location for the test site. It offered excellent flying weather and unparalleled remoteness. The abandoned airfield that Ritland had remembered was totally overgrown and unusable, but the lake-bed was a different story. Bissell later described the hard-packed playa as "a perfect natural landing field ... as smooth as a billiard table without anything being done to it."

Kelly Johnson had originally balked at the choice of Groom Lake because it was farther from Burbank than he would have liked, and because of its proximity to the Nevada Proving Ground (later renamed the Nevada Test Site). Johnson was understandably concerned about conducting a flight test program adjacent to an active nuclear test site. In fact, Groom Lake lay directly in the primary "downwind" path of radioactive fallout from aboveground shots. Johnson obviously didn't understand the full reasoning behind the choice for Groom Lake meaning the research and development on recovered alien craft and artifacts.

Johnson ultimately accepted Ritland's recommendation because AEC security restrictions would help shield the operation from public view. Bissell secured a presidential action adding the Groom Lake area to the AEC proving ground.

During the last week of April, Johnson met with CIA officials in Washington, D.C., and discussed progress on the base and the AQUATONE program. His proposal to name the base "Paradise Ranch" was accepted. It was an ironic choice that, he later admitted, was "a dirty trick to lure workers to the program." The U-2 became known as "The Angel from Paradise Ranch." The base itself was usually just called "The Ranch" by those who worked there.

In May, LeVier, Johnson, and Skunk Works foreman Dorsey Kammerer returned to Groom Lake. Using a compass and surveying equipment, they laid out a 5,000-foot, north-south runway on the southwest corner of the lake-bed. They also staked out a general area for buildings and then flew back to Burbank.

On May 18, 1955, Seth R. Woodruff Jr., Manager of the AEC Las Vegas field office, announced that he had "instructed the Reynolds Electrical and Engineering Co., Inc. [REECo] to begin preliminary work on a small, satellite Nevada Test Site installation." He noted that work was already underway at the location "a few miles northeast of Yucca Flats and within the Las Vegas Bombing and Gunnery Range." Woodruff stated that the installation would include "a runway, dormitories, and a few other buildings for housing equipment." The facility was described as "essentially temporary." The press release was distributed to 18 media outlets in Nevada and Utah including a dozen newspapers, four radio stations, and two television stations. This, in effect was Area 51's public birth announcement.

Watertown, the U-2 and Exotic Technology

CIA, U.S. Air Force, and Lockheed support personnel for the U-2 began arriving in July 1955, and the test site soon acquired a new name. During the 1950s, the site appeared in all official documents as "Watertown." The site was named after Watertown, NY, the birthplace of CIA Director Allen Dulles (Section 2, Chapter 2). To this day, Watertown is listed as a member of Alamo Township in Lincoln County, NV. Dulles also reportedly picked Watertown to do reverse engineering and testing on recovered UFO artifacts like those recovered in the New Mexico desert during July 1947. Tim Cooper's mother related a story from a chemist friend who said she saw none other than Allen Dulles and Albert Einstein together at Area 51 in 1954.

In October 1955, a reporter from the *Las Vegas Review-Journal* requested a progress report on the Watertown project. On 17 October,

Col. Alfred D. Starbird at AEC headquarters issued a statement through Kenner F. Hertford of the Albuquerque Operations Office.
"Construction at the Nevada Test Site installation a few miles north of Yucca Flat which was announced last spring were continuing. Data secured to date has indicated a need for limited additional facilities and modifications of the existing installation. The additional work which will not be completed until sometime in 1956 is being done by the Reynolds Electrical and Engineering Company, Incorporated, under the direction of the Atomic Energy Commission's Las Vegas branch office."

So, publicly there was nothing really secret about the existence of Area 51 in 1955 and immediately there after. What was secret were the details of testing and development of exotic technology and then there were those technologies that "didn't exist." But, by September 1978, Area 51 had disappeared from maps of the NTS produced by the Department of Energy (DOE), but why? Was there a sudden need to test "don't exist" hardware? We can only speculate.

In 1961, it became more apparent that the U-2 would soon be vulnerable to hostile missiles, so the CIA sought a successor that could fly higher and faster and be less visible to radar. Once again, Lockheed was selected to build a new reconnaissance aircraft. The CIA ironically named the project "OXCART." Lockheed's new airplane was designated the "A-12," with the "A" standing for "Archangel."

All 15 A-12 aircraft were initially based at Groom Lake, although some were later deployed to Japan to perform reconnaissance flights over Southeast Asia. While the aircraft were operated by the CIA's 1129th Special Activities Squadron, Lockheed pilots conducted most of the test flights ("Roadrunners").

In that same year, new hangars and housing units were erected. Facilities in the main cantonment area included workshops, buildings for storage and administration, a commissary, control tower, and fire stations. By early 1962, a fuel tank farm was ready for use. Recreational facilities included a gymnasium, movie theatre, nine-hole golf course, and a softball diamond.

Starting in November 1977, there was a succession of what would eventually be publicly acknowledged programs. These included the YF-117A STARS aircraft, the Lockheed SENIOR PROM stealthy cruise missile, Northrop AGM-137 Tri-Service Standoff Attack Missile (TSSAM), McDonnell Douglas/Boeing *"Bird of Prey"* manned technology demonstrator, and various unmanned air vehicles and all operational low-observable U.S. aircraft, to include the F-117A, B-2, and F/A-22A.

Those Saucer Men?

The secret nature of the base has bred rumor and speculation among die-hard UFO believers that the U.S. government was hiding captured extraterrestrial spacecraft, or even aliens (dead and alive) at the site. Such stories have been circulating since at least the late 1970s or the same time frame Groom Lake had disappeared from government maps. Starting in 1989, groups of UFO believers began to camp out near the Nellis Range boundaries near Groom Lake to watch for "flying saucers." The thinking was that if all the rumors about stealth technology and exotic hypersonic aircraft turned out to be true, why not crashed saucers and alien bodies?

By extension, we believe NASA was involved in reverse engineering propulsion work at Watertown (Area 51) since the National Aeronautics and Space Act of 1958 allowed NASA officials and technician's access to restricted data (Atomic Energy Act of 1954). The SOM1-01 document suggests (2) that alien hardware and propulsion items were studied at Site 4, Groom Lake in the 1950s. We know NACA (3) cooperated with the CIA projects at Area 51, and in 1958 Eisenhower signed into law the National Aeronautics and Space Act of 1958 reconstituting NACA (National Advisory Committee for Aeronautics) authorizing the AEC, DOD, and NASA to share restricted data. The Tonopah test range (Nellis AFB) and Papoose Lake range area became part of Groom Lake Area 51 facility (part of the AEC Indian Springs, Nevada Proving Ground) sometime in the late 1950s.

In the reverse engineering of these reported recovered UFOs, the Air Force and others were reportedly required to design our own control systems around the "alien" technology. It was said that the "alien" control and power systems (i.e., Crystal Rectangle) were so far advanced that we had no hope of understanding them even if we were to get a working device within a reasonable amount of time (reference Chapter 3). The power plants were reported to be nuclear because we didn't understand the alien's power system. The Cash Landrum case of December 1980 (last chapter), was said to have been one such reverse-engineered device which had all sorts of problems (4), (5). Comments were made that a few of these reverse-engineered prototypes had been lost in the Gulf of Mexico due to problems with the "black boxes." The black boxes controlled the "anti-gravity force fields" around the device or craft. This is probably one good reason why we still fly space shuttles and their forecasted updates which are still on the drawing board. Each reverse-engineered craft is said to cost up to $5 billion each with a reported total cost of $17 billion, which comes out to be ~ 85 billion in "black funds," quite a hefty hunk of change (6). But, after what our confidential LANL source said in Chapter 3, was it all a waste of money?

Albert Einstein, Robert Oppenheimer and Theodore von Karman were reported to be members of the Scientific Advisory Group who dealt with reverse engineering efforts (See Twining's "White Hot" report (7). Is this is the same "Advisory Group" mentioned by others today in connection with reverse engineering? What's more interesting is a draft report written by Albert Einstein and Robert Oppenheimer in June of 1947 (same month the ED was reportedly recovered, see previous Chapter) (8). This document establishes a UFO connection for both Einstein and Oppenheimer weeks before the reported Roswell crash of July 1947 (refer back to Section 1, Chapter 2). Also, there are reportedly thousands of pages of unreleased notes, letters and papers that belonged to Albert Einstein which are now kept by the Einstein family. Publicly available documents are also available from the Einstein archives online (9).

Private Industry Looking into Gravity Control

From the New York Herald articles of November 1955:

"Private industry is also looking at the question of gravity control with new seriousness. A large number of giant corporations, including Bell Aerospace, General Electric, Hughes Aircraft, Boeing, Douglas and many others, have set up gravity projects." If we are to believe leaders in the field such as Ben Rich, who headed up Lockheed Skunk Works before he died, then we have already developed anti-gravity technology. Just prior to his death, he stated to a small group after a lecture that: "We already have the means to travel among the stars, but these technologies are locked up in black projects and it would take an act of God to ever get them out to benefit humanity...." He went on further to state that, "Anything you can imagine, we already know how to do." Strong words from a knowledgeable deep insider and words that support what a number of witnesses have stated as well (10).

Those Unsolved Mysteries: The Other Half of the Story?

The modern day Area 51 Groom Lake complex contains the cantonment area, runway, buildings, and an extensive underground complex which includes room for nuclear and chemical weapons. Papoose Lake contains an underground structure called the "Sierra Complex," Sierra 1, 2, 3, 4 or "Development Research Complex 4" perhaps for high energy laser testing. Tonopah contains an open air base with facilities. Papoose Mountain has a highly classified communications facility with an antenna farm atop the mountain. The Nevada Test Site (NTS) with its entrance at Mercury contains a set of test areas, buildings and underground facilities. Some of these facilities are old, built or dug in the early '50s; the newer underground facilities were built in the late 1980s-90s. Some of the activities at Area 51 were moved to other sections of the NTS. Indian Springs AFB, located south of Mercury, contains a flight line, fuel depot, flight operations for unmanned aircraft and one underground facility located east of the flight line.

One reported location for the S4 building is west of the main runway at Groom Lake near the base of the mountain. This mountain is at the northern tip of the Papoose Mountain range. S4 is an underground complex with two entrances, one being at the command post and the other near the foot of the mountain through the 4th hanger upper level entrance. Another reported location for S4 is in Papoose Mountain near the southeast corner at the base of the mountain. There are also two entrances to S4 in this case; one on the southeast corner and the other on the east side at the base of the mountain.

The first three levels of S4 are as follows: Level 1 or S4-A is a workstation consisting of laboratories, maintenance bays and equipment storage (Figures 2 and 3). Level 2 or S4-B, is a storage location for the ET craft. Level 3 or S4-C, is a top-secret location and sources do not know what is located on this level. They think advanced propulsion systems are in development. The ground level of this facility has nine (9) hangar doors.

These descriptions fit with what Rick Doty (working out of DIA until 1988), Thomas Mack, now deceased (12), Darren Edmunson (retired AF major who worked for Det 22 AFIS, Air Force Intelligence Service now working in Germany) and other sources have stated concerning this 3 to 4 level facility.

Rick Doty said in July 1999 in reference to Figures 2 and 3: "Yep, matter of fact, it is exactly correct. Great 3D work, I'm not sure about the text info, but the drawing is of S4! Of course, since I had access, I was never escorted. I had free access to the first and second floor. If my memory is correct, there were five floors total. I have never heard of Project Galileo. Could be right, but if it was, I didn't have access to it. I never heard of the medical information Lazar mentioned. I never took any antidote for alien material. I think that stuff is bull. I never had any blood tests at that facility. I had a CIA clearance while there with a special access number, as I recall it was, 00-09-8991432. I was at S4 in 1982, 1983, 1984, and 1987 (11). While there, I wore a badge of light blue with a dark black border. It contained my picture and directly below the picture was a number or 00-34-090. Then below that number was your SSN. There were a series of numbers, written vertically along the left side. I think the numbers went from 11 thru 21. Then next to each number was a box. If you had access to that area, the box was checked. Then along the right side of the badge were the words, "SILVER, GOLD AND AMBER."

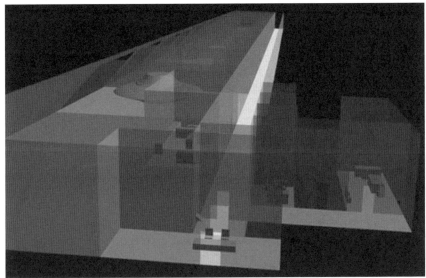

Figure 2: Level 1 side view, S4-A: Courtesy of Bob Lazar

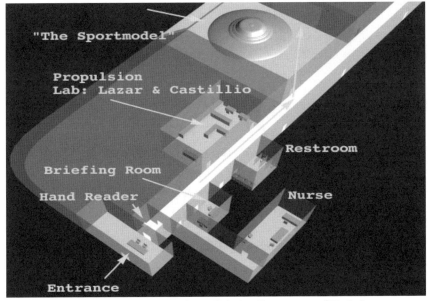

Figure 3: Level 1 top view, S4-A: Courtesy of Bob Lazar

This was related to your security clearance. GOLD was the highest. Horizontal bars were placed next to your security clearance in bold font. We must emphasize here, all activities at Groom Lake are highly compartmentalized.

There is another Site-4 or S-4 located approximately northwest of Groom Lake in the Tonopah test range: This S-4 is not related to the Groom Lake mountain S-4 Complex.

The 9 pop-up type garage doors on the side of this Groom Lake mountain are extremely well camouflaged. Testing is done at night and the reverse-engineered craft (if they are working at the time) do not venture far from the S4 airspace.

For a view of one of these supposed "reverse-engineered" saucers please see the artist rendition in Figure 4 and Figure 5 for an actual model. Figure 4 is termed the "Lazar Sports Model." Although critics and others alike have attempted to discredit Bob Lazar, it seems that Rick Doty plus others have confirmed this "rendition" or "classic UFO" as exactly what they saw while assigned to S4 (the "Desert Disneyland") referenced before.

To add further support for Lazar, there is also Gene Lakes (now in his 80s supposedly) who is a retired Chief of Security at Area 51 (DIA/ASMD) having retired in 1996 from the U.S. Government, and again in 2003 after working seven years for a contractor at the Los Alamos National Laboratory (LANL). Gene's background was checked by Rick Doty and he was found to be authentic. Lazar was said to have had Level II access to Tonopah. He also had Level III access to Groom Lake, meaning, he had to be escorted in and out of the area. He worked on the F117 systems as a civilian according to an access/entry control list for Area 51 that Gene had in his personal possession. Bob Lazar entered Area 51 on 22 occasions, all escorted. His job was associated with propulsion tests conducted either at Papoose Lake or the Nevada Test Site (NTS). Hence, knowing the above, can we conclude that Lazar was used as a government patsy to disclose certain information to the public starting in 1989?

Figure 4

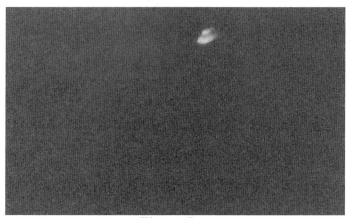

Figure 5

Is the 1990 photo a prototype reverse-engineered saucer over Groom Lake (Figure 5)? Photo was taken by a former colleague of Civilian Intelligence Network, Gary Schultz, on Wednesday, February 28, 1990 just south of Hwy 375 on "Mail Box" Road, looking due south towards Jumbled Hills and Groom Mountains. Object appeared to be an orange light in the distance. Upon development and enlargement, dome and general shape became apparent. A NIKON Action Camera with 1600 ASA film was used.

What Else? A Prepared Statement from Gene Lakes

"Mr. Collins: I am real. Check me out. I worked for the DIA from January 12, 1964 until June 30, 1996. I was a contract employee for LANL from January 1997 until June 2003. I am fully retired. I'm sure Mr. Doty will remember me since we both worked together at KAFB and Tonopah. I was an investigator for the DIA and then director of security operations. You are right about the compartmentalization at site 51. We had several levels of security clearances. SCI/SAR/CCD/FDG/SI/TK/OR/ME. Anyone who worked at Site 51, would know the differences. Military personnel, who were assigned to Site 51 had a different nomenclature attached to their security clearance. As for what we did at the Site 51, well, you'll have to figure that out on your own. I can't give specific details, but we did have some interesting "Craft" that were not of this world. We also had a research program to identify items recovered from UFO crash sites. I was never involved in disinformation. That was left to another division within the DIA. Check with Mr. Doty; he was involved in that division. But I can tell you, without a doubt, that Burisch or Crain, was never employed at the site. There was no "clean room" or special living quarters for visitors. I saw them, had access to them and would have known if they were isolated or quarantined. They were not. None of them got sick or needed special skin cultures from some fictitious person like Burisch or Crain. Burisch was never on any access, at least from Jan 1, 1956 to Sept 30, 2003. I have the lists and his name does not appear on any of them. He never had access to our areas.

"There were levels of clearances and accesses, and yes, everything at A51 was compartmentalized. But some people had access to most, if not all the areas. I had that access. I might not have had access to every bit of classified information, especially technical information regarding specific programs/projects. But I had a working knowledge of them and, if I needed it, I could have had access to the technical information. We had two briefings, every single week of the year.

"There was the Monday morning briefing and the Thursday afternoon briefing. With exception of Thanksgiving, we had the meetings. Everything was discussed. The meetings were code word cleared, simply meaning, everything could be discussed at the meeting. The meetings were held in a secure facility, cleared up to TS code word. I heard some pretty wild things during these meetings. I heard of black projects that were hidden within other black projects that were hidden into other projects–Layered System or (LS)–as we called them, because of the sensitivity of the information or the use of "Visitors" assistance. Now if we had a special sphere or special program to medically examine our visitors, I would have heard about it during these meetings. The DIA and CIA were all present. With exception to "Executive" issues, I attended each meeting. The Executive issues pertained to some extremely sensitive Presidential directives. I can only remember two such sessions, one in 1965 and the other in 1970. Now I did take vacations, and a meeting or two might have taken place during my vacation, but I would have been briefed upon my return.

"Dan Crain/Burisch was never associated with A51–never. The Crain I mentioned was a US Navy scientist, assigned to the scientific intelligence section. This was the same section that Tom Mack and Paul McGovern were assigned to (12).

"I knew every single building and what was located in every single building or facility. I have never seen any special living quarters or "clean sphere" for our visitors. There were numerous clean rooms, but not connected to any living or medical facilities. The visitors lived in one area (S-2): underground. They were guarded and controlled, but did not need any special air or breathing system." Gene Loscowski (Lakes) at: <Gene.Loscowski@gmail.com>

Paul McGovern Weighs in

"Having been very involved in the program for many years, some years before Gene, I know the real story about A51. Gene described it adequately in several past exchanges. I worked with Tom Mack.

Tom was one hell of a great person. He knew his business and he knew it well. He was the Air Force Liaison to the scientific research division. We had a lot of brains at the complex and some were military scientists. Tom was one of the best. I first met Tom in 1975. Tom was TDY to the complex, working on an extraordinary project that he developed. Tom came back in 1976 and stayed for many years before leaving on a Pentagon assignment. Tom again came back in the late '80s and stayed until retirement. He could look at information, clearly not of this world, and just hunch his shoulders and then crack a joke. After Tom retired, we stayed pretty close.

"There was a special office in charge of the information, but it was not responsible for disinformation. That was the responsibility of the DIA. The safeguarding, analysis and distribution of sensitive information was the responsibility of the special office. We had some real Gems at the complex. Matter of fact, I might call it a Gold mine! But, we didn't always understand what we had or how it all worked. We had some foreign help. The little guys helped us and were never a threat to anyone. They mined better than dogs. They never questioned an order, never strayed from their operation zone and never hurt a single thing. They did not need any special sphere or "clean room." All that information from Burisch or Crain is bogus–crap. They were safeguarded from the public and never asked much in return. They were more loyal to us than some of our own people. With their help, we perfected Zero Point Energy (ZPE) technology and magnetic wave coupling.

"Someday the full truth will be told. President Ronald Reagan wanted to disclose the truth but too many advisers wanted the truth, to remain hidden." Paul McGovern at:
<pmcgovernnts@yahoo.com>

A JROD?

Both Gene and Paul would mention a JROD. Paul McGovern would mention JROD as a "controlled visitor." Tom Mack stated that JROD assisted with the reverse-engineering of crashed UFOs

(12). Gene would say the JROD program was highly classified. Is this the same JROD that Dan Burisch or Crain would mention as having medical problems and was contained within a controlled environment called the "clean sphere?" But, both Gene and Paul say there were never any sick aliens and they NEVER heard of a Dan Burisch or Crain (13). JROD was reportedly responsible for the "Gate 3 (NTS) Incident" in April 1983 which involved the murder of a security guard. Rick Doty and Paul McGovern were reported present at the crime scene. The JROD program was terminated in 2002.

Is it time to stop? Not just yet, but we hope that between Chapters 3 and 4, we have made a small but very significant first step in showing a concerted effort by the U.S. government to research, develop and eventually produce a technology based on what they have learned from the recovered alien technology. As we have seen, there are and will be many roadblocks to overcome in the future. As our LANL confidential source has said, "I've worked on this project for 12 years and I sometimes call myself dumb because I try to compare the craft with our technology. Doing that is dumb, as all who have worked on the craft over the years have come to understand." From the horse's mouth, so to speak, the road was not as easy as they thought it might have been way back in 1947.

Project Serpo/ Crystal Knight: An Exchange Program with the Aliens at Area 51-Nevada Test Site?

Between the years 1965 through 1978, we had an exchange program with aliens according to Rick Doty, Ed Doty (Rick's uncle), Gene Loscowski (real last name is Lakes), and Paul McGovern. We carefully selected 12 military personnel; 10 (ten) men and two (2) women. Other sources state that there were only 12 men. They were trained, vetted and carefully removed from the military system. The 12 were skilled in various specialties. There were eight USAF comprised of 6 men and two women or men, two Army and two Navy men. Two were doctors; three were scientists;

two were language specialists; two were security personnel; two were pilots and one was the leader (colonel-AF). The two women or men were one AF major-medical doctor and the other an E-6 linguist.

Near the northern part of the Nevada Test Site, the aliens landed and the 12 Americans left. One entity was left on Earth. The original plan was for our 12 people to stay 10 years and then return to Earth.

But something went wrong. One team member died of a pulmonary embolism enroute to the alien's home world. 11 arrived safely about nine (9) months after departing Earth. The 11 remained until 1978, more than three years beyond the 10 years planned and only seven (7) returned to the same location in Nevada; six men and one woman or man returned. Two others decided to remain according to the returnees, two others had already died on the alien's home planet before the returnees departed. Of the seven who returned, all have died. The last survivor died in 2002.

The returnees were isolated from 1978 through 1984 at various military installations. The Air Force Office of Special Investigation (AFOSI) was responsible for their security and safety. AFOSI also conducted debriefing sessions with the returnees. The complete debriefing is contained in: "PROJECT SERPO," Final Report-80HQD893-020, classified TS, Codeword. The completed SERPO debriefing accounts for about (3,000) three thousand pages. Also, from recent information, it appears that SERPO is the 4th planet from Zeta Reticuli 2. The same planet EBE-1 came from which EBE-1 called "Sieu."

By now, readers will ask themselves, "Haven't I seen this in a movie?" The answer would be "Yes." Steven Spielberg's "Close Encounters of the Third Kind" was based on this reported, supposed real event.

Are all of these sources, stories and documents correct? After 20 years of extensive research we believe this to be the case, but who will pay attention and believe it? Will it be the politics of fear that keep us from the truth? Does Congress even have the courage to address issues like this? Recent and past events cast severe doubt on any government official(s) doing anything publicly. Instead, it seems we will be stuck with "leaks" and at the mercy of those doing the leaking. It is often individuals–not governments–that make the difference, it's bottom up, not top down. We have now come full circle, so where do we begin?

References/Footnotes

(1) Groom Lake was never a secret: http://www.dreamlandresort.com/pete/no_secret.html.

(2) The SOM1-01 document; http://209.132.68.98/pdf/som101_part1.pdf.

(3) NACA, http://naca.larc.nasa.gov/.

(4) Bergstrom AFB interview of Betty Cash, Vickie and Colby Landrum: http://www.cufon.org/cufon/cashlani.htm.

(5) "Diamond in the Sky;" http://ufos.about.com/library/weekly/aa091498.htm?terms=Diamonds+in+the+Sky.

(6) *The Black Budget Report: An Investigation into the CIA's 'Black Budget'* and the *Second Manhattan Projec*t, http://www.american.edu/salla/Articles/BB-CIA.htm.

(7) Twining's "White Hot Report" of 19 September 1947; http://209.132.68.98/pdf/twining_whitehotreport.pdf.

(8) "Relationships with Inhabitants of Celestrial Bodies," http://209.132.68.98/pdf/oppenheimer_einstein.pdf,draft copy, written by Albert Einstein and Robert Oppenheimer, June 1947.

(9) Einstein Archives online, http://www.alberteinstein.info/.

(10) Book review by Hal Puthoff of *Synopsis of Unconventional Flying Objects* by Paul Hill; http://www.nidsci.org/articles/puthoff_bookreview.php.

(11) Bob Lazar: http://www.boblazar.com/

(12) Thomas Mack on Groom Lake; http://www.ufoconspiracy.com/reports/arv.htm

(13) Project Aquarius and the Story of Dr. Dan Burisch; http://www.astrosciences.info/Aquarius.htm

Epilogue

Putting this book together was no easy task. We were often required to work from sketchy information and in many cases there are no references. There has been a great deal of source information presented that in many cases has no verification beyond verifying a few names and places. This book has pushed the frontiers of books related to the UFO subject. Bits and pieces of the information that were presented can be verified and checked including all of the information on Wright-Patterson. My contributor Rick Doty will corroborate all of what he has stated for the record unless he starts having "Regrets" which also applies to the other sources. Research will continue on not only what is contained in the preceding pages, but on new information as well which is being received on a continual basis. However, we must all realize that large volumes of UFO information still remain highly classified and "Exempt from Disclosure."

About the Author, Contributors, Writers and Editor

–Robert M. Collins: A former Air Force Intelligence officer with an extensive background in Aircraft Avionics systems, Ground Communications, and Engineering Physics totaling over 22 years.

–Richard C. Doty: In the spring of 1978, he was recruited by the Air Force Office of Special Investigations (AFOSI) to become a Special Agent. Upon graduating from the academy, he was sent to District 17, OSI, Kirtland AFB, NM in May 1979. During that first year, he was briefed into a special program. The program involved the collection of intelligence and counter-intelligence information for UFOs and "other" foreign intelligence.

–Timothy S. Cooper: As the unwitting focus of much of the investigation into the Majestic-12 documents, Cooper quietly began his investigation into the CIA and NSA's UFO activities in 1988 through FOIA requests. He has received private investigator training and served his country during Vietnam in both the Navy and the Marine Corps. He currently works in private security. Tim can be reached by writing to: P.O. Box 1206, Big Bear Lake, CA 92315. As for Tim Cooper's father see, http://www.ufoconspiracy.com/reports/authors_writers_consultants.htm

Index